W9-CHN-306

Houston, Texas

"I have known and booked Steve Adubato as a passionate voice on a variety of issues and on a variety of shows over the past twenty-plus years. Steve has always been a master communicator and a passionate leader, either in front of the camera or on the front lines of issues. The lessons shared by Steve inside this book are invaluable for anyone leading a team."

—Dave Brown, executive producer, WNET/WLIW (PBS),
    and formerly of CNN and Fox News

"*Lessons in Leadership* might just be the most practical book written on how to influence others, inspire action, and make a difference. This easy-to-read, no-fluff handbook can help you do big things in the world."

—Michael Port, *New York Times* bestselling author of *Steal the Show*

"Steve Adubato perfectly captures the essence of leadership and offers practical lessons that can be used in all aspects of our lives."

—Frank Longobardi, chief executive officer, CohnReznick LLP

"*Lessons in Leadership* offers concrete tools based on real-life scenarios that can help leaders develop the empathy and emotional intelligence to fully understand and motivate their teams' players, confront those who are performing less than optimally, and give constructive feedback, all while owning their own mistakes and embracing any changes necessary to achieve their goals and advance their platforms."

—Patrick C. Dunican Jr., chairman and managing director,
    Gibbons PC

"Drawing from his own experience, Steve Adubato shines a much-needed light on challenges and solutions to create better leaders for tomorrow. Every leader—no matter what industry or position—should read *Lessons in Leadership!*"

—Robert C. Garrett, president and CEO,
    Hackensack University Health Network

"In his book *Lessons in Leadership*, Steve Adubato strikes all the right notes about leading human organizations. First and foremost, these leaders must continually be willing to learn, listen, reflect, have a heart, be humble, empathetic, and optimistic. These leadership characteristics come alive in the book's case studies, an invaluable learning tool. We are proud he is a visiting lecturer at our university."

—Joel Bloom, EdD, president, New Jersey Institute of Technology

"Steve Adubato has effectively captured time-tested methods using real-life experiences to underscore the importance of vision, integrity, trust, and passion to motivate and inspire teamwork. His lessons resonate across all walks of life, bringing great value for all those genuinely interested in understanding the qualities of a true leader."

—Barry H. Ostrowsky, president and CEO, RWJBarnabas Health

"Steve Adubato shares fascinating and real world insights and observations on leadership effectiveness in his new book. *Lessons in Leadership* is a must read for anyone in a leadership position."

—Robert A. Marino, chairman, president, and CEO,
Horizon Blue Cross Blue Shield of NJ

"Steve Adubato's book contains valuable advice on the essence and importance of leadership. He shares great leadership stories and emphasizes the proactive communication plans so necessary for leaders in today's changing world. Plus, he imparts practical ways to sharpen your leadership skills in this process. A great read."

—Jack Mitchell, chairman, Mitchell Stores,
author, *Hug Your Customers, Hug Your People*

"*Lessons in Leadership* is a provocative book on a challenging topic. All who have had the pleasure of working with Steve Adubato know that 'provocative and challenging' are descriptors readily applied to his public television interviews, his writing and his coaching. A must-read for aspiring leaders everywhere."

—Patricia A. Costante, chairman and CEO,
MDAdvantage Insurance Company of New Jersey

"Steve Adubato is an excellent leadership and communication coach. His lessons are invaluable to executives and others in any field looking to motivate and engage key stakeholders."

—Ihor S. Sawczuk, MD, FACS, president,
Hackensack University Medical Center

"Steve Adubato's humble approach to leadership is refreshing and authentic. He provides great advice with real examples and practical application. This book will have you reconsidering the way you lead!"

—Jerry Crowley, GM/VP, Salem Media of New York

"*Lessons in Leadership* is like a fine wine, made from good stories and aged well with life's experiences. Steve Adubato's lessons are ready to be consumed by all who want to be considered a Vintage!"

 —Annette Catino, CEO, QualCare Alliance Networks, Inc.

"With Steve Adubato at our side during critical moments for our organization, he is able to provide 'Lessons in Leadership' that become immediate learning opportunities. His ability to communicate to key stakeholders is invaluable."

 —Raymond Fredericks, president and CEO, JFK Health

"In his book, Steve Adubato explores the importance of life-long learning for leaders and growing the habit of using the world around you as a 'leadership laboratory.' This shift in mindset is truly what propels great leaders to success today. Steve is a living example of this for all of us."

 —B. Kaye Walter, PhD, president, Bergen Community College

"*Lessons in Leadership* is a requisite read for each one of us. Leaders, as are organizations, are called to continue evolving. *Lessons in Leadership* enhances the fundamental understanding of the need to go beyond yesterday's thought leadership and provides profound insight and concrete instruction on how to bring greater value to the organizations, teams, communities, and families to which we belong."

 —Michellene Davis Esq., executive vice president
  and chief corporate affairs officer, RWJBarnabas Health

"In his candid and honest style, Steve Adubato shares 'Lessons in Leadership' that he has learned from observing and interacting with Pope Francis, Governor Christie, and his own father. But what really engages the reader is Steve's ability to dissect his own leadership style and learn from his self-admitted mistakes in order to 'be a strong as well as a constantly improving and developing leader.' That stance makes Steve's book a rarity among the volumes written on leadership and one that has been sorely lacking until now!"

 —Nancy H. Blattner, PhD, president, Caldwell University

"Being a great leader is not only about power and respect—it is about empathy, self-reflection, and admission of our flaws. Steve Adubato does an excellent job exemplifying what it takes to be truly great and how we can embark on our journey to get there."

 —Warren Geller, president and CEO,
  Englewood Hospital and Medical Center

"It's one thing to define a tenet like leadership, but Steve Adubato has taken it to the next level with this thorough exploration of the topic. Through his longtime passion for leadership, Steve has revealed to us a rich understanding of what leadership really is and he gives us lessons on how to employ it in our own lives: in the workplace and at home."

> —Bill Courtney, subject of the Academy Award–winning film *Undefeated*
> and author of *Against the Grain*,
> CEO of Classic American Hardwoods, Inc.

"Just when I thought I knew most everything about leadership, Steve Adubato comes out with a new book that proves me wrong. Learning is a continuous process. Steve's intimate look into the leadership styles and flaws of some of our great leaders is inspiring and thought-provoking."

> —Gary S. Horan, FACHE, president and chief executive officer,
> Trinitas Health and Regional Medical Center

"Steve Adubato has it exactly right! You earn the right to lead others when you start with leading yourself—holding yourself accountable to continually learn and grow and to role model the behaviors that you expect, especially around behaving ethically, authentically, and engendering trust and respect."

> —Lucia DiNapoli Gibbons, executive vice president,
> head of Eastern Business Banking, Wells Fargo

"Steve Adubato has provided great counsel to leaders from all industries during the toughest of circumstances. With this book, everyone can benefit from his years of experience."

> —Stephen K. Jones, chief academic officer,
> RWJBarnabas Health

"Communication, confrontation, self-awareness, self-control, inspiration, passion, finding common ground, visionary innovation, reflection, emotional intelligence, and being able to be realistic and move on—from these threads, and more, Steve Adubato weaves a tapestry of leadership lessons. His stories are compelling; his writing is vintage Steve—accessible, clear, blunt, practical, and wise. Great and aspiring leaders can all learn from this book, which could not be more timely."

> —Maurice J. Elias, PhD, professor of psychology
> at Rutgers University, co-director of the Academy
> for Social-Emotional Learning in Schools,
> and author of *Emotionally Intelligent Parenting*

LESSONS IN LEADERSHIP

LESSONS IN LEADERSHIP

STEVE ADUBATO, PH.D.

Rutgers University Press

New Brunswick, New Jersey, and London

Library of Congress Cataloging-in-Publication Data
Names: Adubato, Steve, author.
Title: Lessons in leadership / Steve Adubato, Ph.D.
Description: New Brunswick, New Jersey : Rutgers University Press, 2016. |
Includes bibliographical references.
Identifiers: LCCN 2015047290| ISBN 9780813580555 (hardcover : alk. paper) |
ISBN 9780813580562 (e-book (epub)) | ISBN 9780813580579 (e-book
(web pdf))
Subjects: LCSH: Leadership.
Classification: LCC HD57.7 .A3165 2016 | DDC 658.4/092—dc23
LC record available at http://lccn.loc.gov/2015047290

A British Cataloging-in-Publication record for this book is available from the
British Library.

Visit our website: http://rutgersuniversitypress.org

Manufactured in the United States of America

*This book is dedicated to my father, Steve Adubato Sr.,
who has taught me a great deal about leadership—the good,
the bad and the sometimes hard to understand.*

*It's also dedicated to all the leaders out there who are working
to make a difference in the lives of others by actively being
in the game every day and not standing on the sidelines.
You are the brave ones who deserve much credit.*

Contents

Preface

One of the most significant lessons in leadership I have learned from my father, Steve Adubato Sr., is about personal courage. It is about standing up to the "angry mob" when taking unpopular positions that you know will result in ridicule or criticism. In my father's case, it was much worse: early in his career, he endured threats of violence (including death threats) against him and those closest to him and a constant fear of reprisal from a variety of dangerous and angry forces. My father was a frustrated public school teacher in the late 1960s who was also involved in local Democratic Party politics in the heavily Italian American North Ward of Newark, New Jersey, where I grew up. At the time, the Democratic Party in the area was influenced, if not controlled, by powerful and entrenched forces with ties to organized crime. Many of those forces were aligned directly with the mayor of Newark, Hugh Addonizio, who would later be convicted of racketeering and taking bribes and would ultimately be sent to prison for being controlled by and "on the take" with the Mafia.

As a leader, my father chose to challenge the political status quo in Newark and attempted to take over the Democratic Party in this section of the city from a party boss controlled by the Mob. He was told, in no uncertain terms, that doing so would not be smart as it could result in physical violence against him and would not be a good career move. Undaunted, in 1969, my father organized a group to run against the local chairman of the Democratic Party and, after a series of volatile elections in which police had to be called in (police that some believed were aligned with some of the same corrupt forces leading the city administration), my father succeeded in wrestling control of the party.

Immediately thereafter, my father refused to support then indicted Mayor Addonizio for reelection. He instead welcomed the candidacy of Ken Gibson, an African American (which was unheard of in our virtually all-Italian and all-White neighborhood) who, in 1970, would become the first African American mayor of a city on the Eastern Seaboard. There was a strong anti-Black vigilante movement in our neighborhood led by a group of Italian Americans who felt that my father was "betraying our people" for supporting a Black candidate. I remember the death threats against my father that would come in the form of phone calls, pamphlets, and late-night visits from thugs. It would only get worse over time. My father would rarely travel alone as it was made clear to him that, as the local Democratic leader in our section of Newark, he was expected to support the Italian American incumbent mayor—even if this mayor was likely to go to jail.

I remember going to school during the 1970 campaign for mayor, and how on a regular basis many other White kids would say to me, "What's the matter with your father? What is he, some sort of N-lover?" As the election got closer, it happened more and more. Part of me wanted to defend my father, which would cause me to get into many arguments and some fights. Yet, there was another side of me—that, frankly, was much stronger at the time—that kept thinking; "What *is* wrong with my father? Why can't he just go along like all the other Italian American fathers in the neighborhood and support the White mayor—corrupt or not?" I remember going to my father and asking him why he was doing all this. I also remember him being put off by my questioning him—as if I had the nerve to even ask. I could sense that he was angry that I was afraid of not being popular with or liked by the other kids in the neighborhood and that I felt what he was doing was making my life more difficult. He would never really explain the situation to me, as if I was supposed to understand the concept of doing the right thing or having the integrity and courage to stand up. It was a lesson in leadership that I think he thought I should have understood.

Yet, at the time, all I could think of was how, virtually, every day somebody in the neighborhood was telling me something terrible about my father. On some level, I was actually kind of embarrassed of my father, and it would only be years later that I would come to understand the ultimate lesson in leadership about what he did, why he did it, and why he was so courageous. No matter how many people gave me a hard time or went against my father, he was not the type of leader that would go along just to get along. Rather, he stood up for what he believed was right. When I look back I'm somewhat ashamed of the emotions I felt, but then again, I was just a kid.

It all culminated for me one day when I was coming home from school and had forgotten my key. I remember I went to climb into the window of our house and, as I approached, I saw a series of holes in the glass. At first, it wasn't clear to me what I was looking at but I soon realized the holes—bullet holes—were right where my father's chair was located where he sat to watch TV. I ran to a neighbor's house for help tracking my mother down, and for the remainder of the 1970 election, my two sisters and I were shipped out of our home to live with relatives in a town nearby. All the while, my father continued the fight and campaign against a corrupt Mafia-supported Italian American mayor whom everyone else in the neighborhood supported because "at least he was one of our own."

After Ken Gibson became mayor, my father created and built an extraordinary not-for-profit called the North Ward Center, which helped thousands of working-class and poor people in the Newark community I grew up in. It started with ethnic Whites and then branched out to Hispanics and Blacks. He created high school equivalency programs and college placement programs. He helped kids pursue higher education—kids who never even thought it was possible—by finding them financial aid. He built a daycare center so that single mothers who were working or were in school could have a safe place for their children. Later, he founded and built one of the most successful charter schools in the nation, the Robert Treat Academy. He doubled down by building a charter school in the Central Ward of Newark called the Robert Treat Academy Charter School–Jackie Robinson Campus named after one of his heroes, the great Jackie Robinson of the Brooklyn Dodgers. My father's not-for-profit programs would include the creation of new baseball fields for thousands of kids who had previously only played baseball on playgrounds or on rundown fields. He also created countless job-training and employment initiatives. My father took the political power and influence that arose from his challenging the status quo in the late 1960s and early 1970s and parlayed it into a national model for a nonprofit organization that would become recognized for those it served and how it served them.

I share this story about my father because it would be replicated time and time again in which I saw him stand up to an angry mob, go against the tide, lead a cause that he thought was right no matter what those around him thought was the "popular" thing to do. For all my father's faults as a leader, when it came to his tone or demeanor or the fact that he could be incredibly degrading and insulting if he thought you "screwed up" or pissed him off (which I talk about extensively in the pages of this book that follow as a major influence in the not-so-great leadership traits I've learned from him), he is by far the most personally courageous leader I've ever met in my life. He is far more courageous than I could ever hope to be.

The truly exceptional leadership lesson he taught me was that the greatest failure of a leader is not in being afraid (he would often tell me that he was afraid of what could happen to him or those closest to him); rather, the only failure of a leader is ultimately folding in the face of that fear. Failure, my father would say, is letting the fear get the best of you and cause you to cower and give into it. It's doing nothing. Going along. Giving up your principles just so you could feel safer for the moment—at least in your mind.

It's funny, leaders are complex. That's probably because human beings are so complex. We're flawed. We're multifaceted. We're good and bad. We're anything but black-and-white. That is my father. My father used to say, from as far back as I could remember, that when he died he wanted it said on his tombstone: "Steve Adubato . . . he was *not* a nice guy." The first time he said this to me I must have been about twelve years old. It freaked me out. When I finally got the nerve to ask him why he wanted this, he went into a dissertation about how "nice people" don't get anything done and how they "go along and try to get people to like them."

My father really believed that. He probably still believes it today as he's turning eighty-three years old and is dealing with some serious health problems that have taken away his ability to speak, engage, and lead in the way I know he would like to. But while my father was never really a "nice guy," he always had a sense of compassion and a bigger-picture, societal sense of right and wrong. He had a sense of integrity and social justice. No, he wasn't always "nice" to the people closest to him, but he was almost always courageous. It took amazing courage to take on the local party bosses with ties to the Mob in our heavily Italian American neighborhood. It took great courage to stand up and speak up for a Black man running for mayor against racist and violent vigilante forces throughout our own community who would turn on him and everyone around him for it. But he knew it was the right thing, at the right time, for the right reasons, and he was convinced that being "nice" wasn't going to get the job done.

No, my father, Steve Adubato Sr., wasn't always a "nice" guy as a leader, but he was and is courageous and brave in ways that his son can only hope to be one day.

Acknowledgments

Writing a book is never easy and an author never does it alone. He or she needs the help of some talented people. Writing *Lessons in Leadership* has been a product of my being surrounded by excellent team members and leaders in their own right. Most importantly, the team at Stand & Deliver, our leadership development and executive coaching firm, has been critical in the development of this book. Mary Gamba, our VP of Marketing and Client Relations, has helped keep me on track and on schedule but has also developed exceptional relationships with the clients we try to serve every day. She has taught me to be a better leader and has helped me help our clients in ways that I could never have done alone. She has also helped me be a better and more patient leader with our team by giving me constructive and candid feedback—something every CEO needs. The fruit of those efforts is reflected in the pages that follow. A new member of our team, Victoria Eisenstein, has added something really special to the writing process. This is the first time I've worked with Victoria in a writing collaboration, after authoring four books. Such a collaboration with a writing colleague and editor is challenging and sometimes risky. However, with Victoria it's been an absolute pleasure. She is smart, talented, and has consistently challenged me to be a better writer and, in the process, a better leader. This book could never have been written without her and for that I thank her and am extremely grateful. (P.S. Victoria also has the patience of a saint.)

Further, to the team at the Caucus Educational Corporation, the public television production company of which I am proud to serve as CEO, I say thank you for allowing me to lead such a great organization with such committed, hardworking professionals. I especially want to thank our organization's VP of Marketing and Public Relations, Laura Van Bloem, who has been instrumental in the creation of the "Lessons in Leadership" multimedia platform as well as in the final editing of this book.

In addition, because so many of the case studies and examples in the Lessons in Leadership platform, including this book, come from our firm's work, leading seminars and conducting executive coaching for a variety of organizations on the subject of leadership, I have to thank all of the clients at Stand & Deliver who have put their trust in me and our firm to help make a difference for them and their organizations. I never take for granted when an organization agrees to an engagement in which I am asked to coach and develop their professionals in an effort to help them become better leaders. It is an honor and a privilege that continues to be humbling for me, both professionally and personally. Further, it is through that work as a leadership coach that I have learned so many "lessons in leadership" that I have tried to share with other leaders in the pages that follow.

I would also like to thank the hundreds of leaders in a variety of professional arenas who have allowed me, in my capacity as an anchor on public television (more specifically, with our partners WNET, the PBS flagship station in New York, and NJTV, New Jersey's public television station) to ask them about their leadership lessons and challenges, which are reflected in this book. I have learned so much over the past year through those conversations, and I'm confident you will learn as well by reading this book.

I also want to thank my longtime literary mentor and friend at Rutgers University Press, Marlie Wasserman, who continues to believe in my writing and my work in the field of leadership and, in the past, the related field of communication. Marlie is a great leader and has never been shy about giving me very direct feedback, which has always helped me be a better author in the process. For that, I owe her a deep debt of gratitude.

Finally, I'd like to thank our terrific children, Nick, thirteen; Chris, eleven; and Olivia, who is five years old. While I'm not the actual leader of our house, we work together every day with the family's real leader, my wife, Jennifer, to be the best team we can be. I also want to thank Jen for her understanding, once again, of my absurdly long and very odd hours that it took to write another book and my habit of leaving chapter drafts all over our house over these many months. I also want to thank my oldest son, Stephen, now twenty-three, who is teaching in an all-boys urban high school and is attempting to be the best leader he can be in a very challenging environment. I'm so proud of him, as I am of all of my children. I know I'm blessed many times over.

I'm also blessed to be able to do what I love every day. In addition to my broadcasting work, I've been able to teach, coach, and write about leadership—a subject I care deeply about. I'm also fortunate enough to, ultimately, have people like you reading this book and hopefully finding value in it. Professionally, there aren't many things in life better than that.

LESSONS IN LEADERSHIP

Introduction

I've dedicated most of my professional life to trying to master the art of leadership as an author, broadcaster, and motivational speaker as well as appearing on a variety of national media networks as a contributing analyst and commentator over many years. Yet, I still make the most basic leadership mistakes. But I know I continue to learn from these mistakes and hopefully get better in the process. Leadership is funny that way.

While the leadership journey can be fascinating and enlightening, it can also be extremely frustrating. As leaders, why do we have so much difficulty getting our message across to others when the stakes are so high? Why is it sometimes so difficult to manage our emotions as leaders when circumstances and situations frustrate us? It doesn't matter if it involves a situation in the workplace or one with your spouse, child, parent, or sibling; getting the leadership game right is never easy. One of the most powerful and sometimes painful lessons I've learned about leadership is that you must be a leader of yourself before you can dare to be a leader of others. Self-control and self-awareness are essential traits to becoming a great leader. Learning not to be defensive when we screw up and owning our mistakes is also something that fascinates me. What about you?

Why is it so hard to really listen and be present in an age where social media and handheld devices seem to consume every second of our lives? And why do those of us in leadership positions, even though we know intellectually the best way to handle a particular situation with a team member, often overreact or simply blow it and are then only able to see the mistake we made when the dust clears? Or worse, why is it that some leaders can't or won't even see their mistake because of stubbornness, ego, or hubris? Pride, not to mention narcissism, can work for or against us as leaders.

Lessons in Leadership calls attention to some very important and relevant subjects and analyzes the impact our leadership style has on our ability to persuade and motivate those around us. Over the nearly ten years since I wrote *Make the Connection*, published by Rutgers University Press in 2006, I've learned so much more, not just from my work in the field of leadership, but from my everyday experiences in life as a CEO, husband, father, and friend. That's the amazing thing about leadership. Once you think you've got it right or have perfected it, that's when you know you're probably in trouble, because there is no such thing as leadership perfection and you're likely to miss something out of a false sense of confidence or, worse, arrogance. It's clear: the truly great leaders are the ones who are committed to being lifelong learners, using every experience and interaction as an opportunity to pick up a new tip or tool or lesson on what to do and what not to do as they face another challenge.

Further, when you choose to look at the world around you as a leadership laboratory, as I've tried to do, you also begin to see everything that occurs as a potential case study that can teach you powerful lessons. So whether it is the federal government's botched leadership and execution of the launch of the Affordable Care Act website (HealthCare.gov)—and to a significant degree, how President Barack Obama fell short as a leader by not being as engaged in the details as he needed to be—or the 2016 presidential campaign and the spectacle of Donald Trump engaging in insults and name-calling, with millions of Americans confusing that with real leadership, you realize that there are lessons to be learned in many situations. Further, another leadership case to examine from the 2016 presidential race explored in this book involves former secretary of state Hillary Clinton and her inability or outright refusal to simply apologize and admit her mistakes involving her use of a private e-mail server until, for many including me, it was simply too late and she was forced into it. In this book, I argue that this inability or unwillingness to own your mistakes, admit them, and simply say "I was wrong and I apologize" is a leadership flaw Hillary Clinton, Donald Trump, and many others in high-profile positions featured in this book suffer from.

We can also learn leadership lessons from the "Deflategate" controversy involving star NFL quarterback Tom Brady, as well as the case of the *Costa Concordia* cruise ship and its captain, who abandoned ship to save himself instead of looking out for the safety of his passengers. These are two powerful case studies examined in the pages that follow. Why *do* such high-level professionals and so-called leaders make such dumb mistakes? What *were* they thinking (to quote the title of one of my previous books)? Or were they thinking at all? And what price do they pay when they act without thinking or act out of a distorted and misplaced sense of the greater good?

For the purposes of this book, I have outlined what the rest of us, regardless of our professional status or field, can take away from the leadership mistakes of others. Conversely, what about those who get it right? I profile how President John F. Kennedy got it terribly wrong as a leader in the Bay of Pigs fiasco in Cuba in 1961 but, fortunately, got it right during the Cuban Missile Crisis less than one year later, as the world held its breath and was, ultimately, able to breathe a sigh of relief. I also talk about former Yankees manager Joe Torre who, in an in-depth interview with me, explained how he came to understand each Yankees player and what he needed to do to motivate them at critical moments in a game.

Consider General Colin Powell, who also told me in an interview that leaders sometimes need to "piss people off" in order to make it clear that an employee was not performing effectively enough. So many leaders are afraid or unable to confront employees who aren't getting the job done and, in turn, negatively affect their team or organization. *Lessons in Leadership* delves deeper into General Powell's unorthodox yet insightful advice and why it is so valuable to so many. We explore the importance of and lessons surrounding the art of effective confrontation that every leader should understand. We examine the need for leaders to get the poor performers "off the bus," as leadership guru Jim Collins says, as well as the need to keep other people engaged and "pumped up" in the workplace by finding new ways to motivate them.

There is also a section in this book on inspirational leaders and powerful speeches by legendary sports and public figures who are no longer with us, such as former New York governor Mario Cuomo, Yankees icon Lou Gehrig, and North Carolina State University basketball coach Jim Valvano. Lou Gehrig, dying from ALS, called himself "the luckiest man on the face of the earth" in front of a packed house at Yankee Stadium, and thanked everyone from his teammates and managers to the Yankees ball boy with humility and dignity. He emerged as an inspiration to millions and generations to come. What enabled Lou Gehrig, never known to be an outspoken leader, to connect in this way without reading from notes or a prepared text? What causes some people to rise to an occasion bigger than they could imagine and become inspirational leaders and iconic figures in the process? We will explore this question.

Consider when Jim Valvano, coach of North Carolina State, who was in the final stages of bone cancer and spoke at the first televised ESPY Awards about "never giving up." It had nothing to do with sports and everything to do with life and appreciating every moment we have on this earth as well as making a difference in the lives of others. It was also a powerful lesson in leadership that has had a major impact on me as well as millions of others. Jim Valvano and Lou Gehrig knew their days were numbered, but even in their dire physical states, they moved so many people with their words, passion, and conviction. Passion and conviction—two traits every inspirational leader must possess, yet why do these men and their respective speeches in their final days still resonate today? What can the rest of us take from them, why do their speeches matter so many years later, and how can we incorporate our passion and convictions into our leadership approach? That's a lot of what this book explores.

Lessons in Leadership also examines the complex phenomena of mergers and acquisitions. What are the best ways to lead when bringing organizations together, knowing that major changes and potential job losses are on the horizon? How much information should leaders share about the merger and how much should they keep close to the vest? What about the best way to lead the integration of two very different organizations with their own separate and unique cultures, all while employees are feeling fearful, insecure, distrustful of each other, and worried about their futures? This book additionally explores succession planning and how to work successfully to identify and develop the team members who will lead the organization forward into the future. This is no easy task, and my leadership consulting and coaching over the past two decades has taught me that in most organizations, people at the top don't do a very good job in this arena, with serious consequences. Yet, when succession planning is done well—and I've seen it— the benefits are tangible and significant. I share these lessons I've learned, and I'm confident readers will benefit from them.

Lessons in Leadership looks at practical, skill-driven areas such as conducting meetings, listening, presenting, and the art of asking questions. How leaders facilitate meetings matters. It impacts the degree to which they engage team members or not. It also affects the ability of leaders to get things done and reveals how they allow others to speak up and step up and lead themselves. On the listening front, I explore the importance of leaders being open to other points of view and caring enough to be present and not only hear what is being said but actively listen. With so many distractions and contending agendas—not to mention iPhones or whatever handheld device you're using at the moment—competing for a leader's attention, being an engaged and active listener is no easy task. Yet for a leader, listening remains an absolutely essential skill and is more important than ever.

Further, the art of asking questions is an area I've become fascinated by. Great leaders need to understand that the questions they ask or don't ask greatly impact the conversations they have with others around them. This in turn affects their relationships and their ability to achieve organizational goals and navigate difficult and uncertain times. This book shares key tips for asking questions that will get people talking, which is critical to a leader's ability to understand more about where another individual stands or an entire audience is coming from. Artful question asking is crucial to a leader's ability to be more empathetic, which is another powerful and important theme covered in this book.

Related to the topic of empathy is the broader subject of emotional intelligence, or EQ, a term coined by Dr. Daniel Goleman. Emotional intelligence is essential to a leader's ability to understand the complex dynamics of human relationships and is explored in depth in *Lessons in Leadership*. Further, a leader's ability to maintain a positive attitude—even when things go wrong—is vital for success, and this book will help readers understand that "attitude is everything" in many circumstances.

Lessons in Leadership delves into other skills that are essential to a leader's success, such as the ability to give constructive feedback as well as to have the confidence and the maturity to receive it— even when it hurts. People often say that business "is not personal." Yet, when we hear feedback that is negative, or when we fall short or fail as leaders, do we not take any part of this personally? I know I do. In one chapter of this book, I talk about the need for leaders to understand that beyond the importance of thinking about profits and losses, we are dealing with people and their lives. What's more personal than that? In *Lessons in Leadership*, we explore the delicate balance between being clear-headed and objective in our decision making as leaders and doing so with a human touch.

In this book, I explore the need for all of us as leaders to be more self-reflective and, at times, self-critical. We need to constantly strive to be our better self. Again, this is no easy task. I write about leaders like Pope Francis, who as an early leader made significant mistakes by self-admittedly being too dictatorial, to the point of failing miserably. Yet, to his significant credit, Pope Francis, while exiled by the Vatican, decided to become a very different type of leader. He used that time in exile, and had both the courage and innate understanding of himself, to ultimately change his demeanor and overall style of leadership. Demeanor is a topic I explore in great depth in this book, and it is significant to note that Pope Francis returned years later and dedicated his life to the Catholic Church as a more humble servant—a very different type of leader. Much of the pope's popularity today is a product of this decision and his ability to "lead himself" in a very different way. In this chapter, I also disclose my own journey and significant struggle to "lead myself" and manage my emotions more effectively. I assure you: writing about this was not easy. But I am confident that doing so contributed to the lessons in leadership in this book. In fact, part of it was very painful, as I reminded myself of how my sometimes irrational demeanor and aggressive style too often caused unnecessary conflicts with those around me and produced outcomes that were anything but what I was looking for.

I also examine the many leadership lessons I learned from my father, who achieved many great things and impacted many peoples' lives as leader of a nationally recognized not-for-profit organization—yet often did so by leading with an "iron fist." Leading himself and managing his emotions was never a priority for my father, and being introspective was something he was convinced was a waste of time because he was too busy moving forward and achieving great things. Yes, those accomplishments are legendary. You can Google him under "Steve Adubato Sr." and the proof is right there. Yet, what is also legendary to those who were around him was the fear that people felt when in his presence. Often, this leadership approach was necessary to accomplish things in a very difficult and combative environment, not just in the city of Newark where he was based but across the state and the nation as he branched out. Yet, from my perspective, too often and without provocation, the emotional outbursts and the need to create fear and intimidate others was not only unwarranted but unhealthy.

I used to try to talk to him about it and "coach" him, which is laughable if you know my father and know how strong-willed he was when he was actively leading and building the North Ward Center and later the Robert Treat Academy Charter School and other affiliated organizations. Although I was convinced for years that as a leader I wasn't like my father, in the process of writing this book, it has become more clear to me than ever that in certain ways I will always be my father's son, both good and bad. This book examines what I have tried to do, not just to replicate all the positives that I learned from my father as a leader but also to undo the things I've learned from him as a leader that have affected and infected my professional life in leadership positions. (The preface to this book offers a full appreciation of the qualities that have made my father such a great and courageous leader. You see, leadership, like people, isn't black-and-white. It's a very complex equation.)

With respect to leadership demeanor, I explore this issue with New Jersey governor Chris Christie, whose demeanor has become a topic of interest to many. I asked the governor about his demeanor and aggressive "in your face" approach to leadership as well as the legendary "sit down and shut up" video that went viral when he confronted a protestor at a Jersey Shore press conference. While Christie is one of the most gifted and engaging political figures on the scene, this book explores the public television interview I had with the governor in which I asked him if he had any intent of softening or changing his aggressive demeanor as he introduced himself to the nation as a presidential candidate. The governor's response, as always, was candid and revealing. You'll have to turn the pages of this book to find out exactly what he said and why it matters to leaders of all stripes.

Finally, *Lessons in Leadership* offers concrete and useful tips and tools based on real-life scenarios that will help all leaders, regardless of where they fit in an organization chart. The goal of this book is to help you improve your performance as a leader, which will in turn have a positive impact on the overall effectiveness of your team. *Lessons in Leadership* will encourage you to ask some tough questions of yourself and your style as a leader. For example, how do you lead or embrace change within your organization? What unique leadership attributes do you bring to your team? And what are you doing to contribute to a supportive environment that is conducive to team building? How do you lead when things go well? Do you take most of the credit or spread it around? Conversely, how do you lead when things go wrong? Are you quick to blame others, pass the buck, throw a direct report or colleague under the bus? Or do you look in the mirror and ask how you must step up as the team leader and take overall responsibility for the outcome?

These are some of the important and multifaceted questions that will guide you to becoming the most effective leader possible and the ones I think about on a regular basis as a leadership coach and consultant to clients who work in the fields of law, accounting, banking, healthcare, insurance, and higher education. They are also some of the questions and challenges I have posed over the years to my graduate students at various institutions of higher learning where I have been honored to teach, including New York University, Rutgers University, the New Jersey Institute of Technology, Seton Hall University, and Montclair State University. Further, I ask these same questions of many leaders of every stripe as an interviewer for public broadcasting. In fact, the first chapter in this book reveals the responses of dozens of leaders to two important questions. The first question asks prominent leaders to identify the most important leadership lesson they've learned, while the second examines the most pressing leadership challenge they have faced. What I got back, what you will read in the pages that follow, is powerful, revealing, and always candid. None of it was rehearsed. Not one leader I interviewed knew the question was coming beforehand. And so, they "spoke from the heart" (a reference to the title of my first book). I promise you the lessons that you will learn from what these leaders shared with me will have a lasting impact.

But who am I to dish out all this leadership advice? Since *Make the Connection: Improve Your Communication at Work and at Home* was published in 2006, I have written well over 500 columns, essays, articles, and blog posts on the complex subject of leadership and a variety of related topics. I've also facilitated hundreds of seminars and workshops on, and delivered speeches about, leadership and received countless e-mails and letters from people from every walk of life, asking questions and raising issues about how to get their message across more effectively when dealing with challenging and difficult leadership situations as well as in everyday life. I have been privileged to interview dozens of CEOs, executives, and other leaders in all kinds of organizations about how to deal with people, as well as their unique organizational and industry challenges, in my role as a broadcaster with Thirteen/WNET, the PBS flagship station in New York; and NJTV, the public television station in New Jersey. In addition, I often offer leadership analysis and commentary as a contributing analyst on a variety of national broadcast platforms such as NBC's *Today Show*, CNN, Fox News, and NPR.

I'm absolutely convinced—after writing four books on leadership and the related topics of communication and branding, as well as being a longtime columnist for the *Star-Ledger* and, most recently, sharing my own *Lessons in Leadership* syndicated blog through numerous print and online platforms, including NJ.com, *New Jersey Business Magazine*, NJBmagazine.com, NJBIA.org, NJBiz.com, PolitickerNJ.com, AM970TheAnswer.com, CIANJ.org, *Meadowlands USA Magazine*, and MeadowlandsUSA.com—there is still so much more to learn and understand about how leadership really works . . . and doesn't work.

A former editor at the *Star-Ledger* once asked me if it was difficult to come up with a weekly column on leadership and related topics after more than fifteen years of doing so. My response to him represents a major reason for writing this book. The fact is I never seem to run out of fascinating challenges and issues to think about involving leadership. They are all around us in our everyday lives—at work and at home, in our relationships, in our struggles to connect and deal with those around us. The effort to lead others or to lead ourselves in a smarter, more strategic fashion—that is what this book is all about. No matter what you do professionally or where you find yourself in life, to be effective, you must be a strong as well as a constantly improving and developing leader. I have been challenged, motivated, and inspired, yet also humbled in my efforts to try to become a better leader and help others in their efforts as well. I am confident that *Lessons in Leadership* will help you with valuable leadership tips and tools along the way. So, do I find it difficult to come up with leadership topics to write about? Are you kidding me? I'm just getting started. Read on . . .

1

Leadership Lessons from Leaders of All Stripes

Writing this book over the past year has been a fascinating experience: it's not only challenged me to think about how I view leadership—not just in theory but in practice—but it's also given me the unique opportunity to ask hundreds of other leaders how they view leadership. Because one thing *I've* learned is that you can always learn something new about how to lead from someone else by keeping your ears and your mind open. In that spirit, I decided to take advantage of my position as an anchor and interviewer in public broadcasting who interacts with leaders of all stripes to ask two critical questions that have been instrumental in the chapter you are about to read.

The first question I asked was "What is the number-one leadership lesson you've learned?" The second asked these leaders to explore the number-one leadership challenge they have faced. I have been amazed at the range of responses. Keep in mind that none of these leaders were told beforehand that the questions were coming. None were prepped. I asked the questions on the spot, out of the blue and virtually every leader, without hesitation, provided a valuable answer. This chapter takes the most compelling lessons from those interviews and shares powerful insights that I'm confident will be of great value to you and your work as a leader, regardless of the field you are in.

"Never take anything for granted. Sometimes you rise up in an organization and you do not realize the impact that you can have on people. Make sure that every single day you're giving quality time to those people and that you're listening to them. Leaders must mentor the next generation because they are our future."

Frank P. Longobardi, CEO,
CohnReznick, LLP

"Empowering others is a way to expand your power. Surround yourself with competent, trustworthy, and committed people, and let them do their jobs."

Edward Richardson, executive director,
New Jersey Education Association

"Listen to as many people within the organization as you can. Don't let your confidence in your own judgment and decision making overtake the value of the information you can get from the people who are working with you. The 'rank and file' have great ideas, and if you don't listen, you shortcut the advantages that you would ordinarily get as a leader."

Barry H. Ostrowsky, president and CEO,
RWJBarnabas Health

"Humility. You're only as good as the people around you. No one leader can do it all on their own, and in order to keep people engaged you can't be autocratic, you can't be dictatorial, you can't know it all. So, therefore, you also better listen."

Joel Bloom, EdD, president,
New Jersey Institute of Technology

"If you have a sound strategy, if you believe in your strategy and your vision, stick with it. Persistence is key. Don't get sidetracked if at first it's not successful."

Robert C. Garrett, president and CEO,
Hackensack University Health Network

"Relentless follow-up is the most effective leadership best practice I have observed. Successful leaders never cease to push, cajole, encourage, and inspire. Persistence and perseverance are essential to a successful ultimate outcome."

Patrick C. Dunican Jr., chairman and
managing director, Gibbons PC

"Leadership is about integrity, being true to who you are, and believing in your people, your staff, and your company. I've also learned that it's really about controlling one's ego. It's about humility and understanding that we're all people and we all have the same basic human needs."

Robert A. Marino, chairman, president, and CEO,
Horizon Blue Cross Blue Shield of New Jersey

"Never ask anyone to do something you wouldn't do yourself. . . . The key is to lead by example and remember the golden rule—treat other people the way you would want to be treated—because great generals lead from the front, never from the back."

Gerald H. Lipkin, chairman, president,
and CEO, Valley National Bank

"Listen. You can't be a good giver if you don't listen with an open heart and try to understand the needs of others. That kind of deep empathy only comes from listening."

Angelica Berrie, president,
The Russell Berrie Foundation

"Leadership is tough—the issues are harder than ever. It's about getting in front and in many cases going against the tide. As a leader, you must know the terrain, where you are going, and how you are going to take your people there."

Maria Bartiromo, anchor and global markets editor, Fox Business Network

"I've learned to keep compassion as an element of my decision-making process. In today's hyper-capitalistic world, we cannot forget that business decisions often impact human beings and their families. Using your conscience as a barometer does not have to be in opposition with creating value for investors. It is a matter of commitment to character."

Joseph Berardo Jr., chairman, MagnaCare

"Stay true to your principles, and help those behind you as others helped you get where you are. I've been the beneficiary of many mentors, and I've also had the privilege of helping many others. There's nothing better than helping others succeed."

Bruce I. Goldstein, Esq., chair, board of trustees, NJ Sharing Network

"There are three things I try to live by. One, make sure that you learn from the lessons you've had in the past. Two, you're not going to remember everything you've learned in a book, so learn from the street as well. And three, stop every once in a while and celebrate, because too often leaders are yelling and screaming about making a change but they don't celebrate the successes."

Ralph LaRossa, president and COO, PSE&G

"It's okay to admit when you are wrong or fail; the important part is how you pick yourself up and adjust so that it doesn't happen again. Also, you can't fix things that you don't know are broken. Encourage your team to bring you problems, but they should always come with suggested solutions."

D. Nicholas Miceli, market president, TD Bank

"Create a culture where everyone feels like they're part of what happens. That they own a piece of the success of the organization and that they'll be celebrated for that."

Patricia A. Costante, chairman and CEO,
MDAdvantage Insurance Company of New Jersey

"Listen. The ability to hear and listen emphatically to what people are *really* saying is critical. When you listen to what's going on, you can really get to someone's heart and truly understand what's important to them."

Michael J. Smith, president, Berkeley College

"I learned over time to try not to just focus on problem-solving related to poor performance or results. You need to also focus on times when the results are spectacular and study how the organization achieved the high performance. Then, those learnings can be used to hard-wire the competencies for even greater results and apply them to the problem areas—along with recognizing those responsible and celebrating."

Kevin J. Slavin, president and CEO,
St. Joseph's Healthcare System

"Don't overreact to initial reports or information. Verify the facts with trusted resources and then put together your plan of attack."

Annette Catino, CEO, QualCare Alliance Networks, Inc.

"Leadership is all about people. Surround yourself with the most competent and talented individuals. It is easily said, but hard to do."

John K. Lloyd, FACHE, president and CEO, Meridian Health

"The foundation of a good leader is to be human first and to be a manager second. If you treat the decisions you make as a manager from a human perspective first, it will have a long-term impact on the culture of the organization and the people you are serving."

Rodger L. DeRose, president and CEO, Kessler Foundation

"Invest in your people. Make sure that you're training them, that you have employees who are motivated and eager to do the job for your customers."

Ralph Izzo, chairman of the board, president, and CEO, PSEG

"Treat everyone the way you want to be treated. Also, when in a position of power, use that power appropriately and help the people who don't have a voice."

Becky Quick, co-anchor, *Squawk Box*, CNBC

"Life is precious and life is short. You have to be an active participant. You need to be engaged, and those of us who have the ability also have a responsibility to take care of and look out for those who are less fortunate."

Michael Maron, president and CEO, Holy Name Medical Center

"A leader has to be there 24/7. It's about the mentality of always being with your people all the time, being present, being positive, and being proactive."

Jack Mitchell, author, *Hug Your Customers* and *Hug Your People*; chairman, Mitchell Stores

"Encourage an environment where credit is shared but responsibility is accepted. Do not let team members compete, via either a lack of identifying the contributions of other team members or the placing of blame for mistake. Discourage the use of the pronoun 'I' to engender a greater sense of team collaboration among staff."

Michellene Davis, Esq., executive vice president and chief corporate affairs officer, RWJBarnabas Health

"Surround yourself with good people. Listen to them and let them make decisions—don't make decisions for them. It's important to find the right people who have the subject-matter expertise and really rely on them."

Robert H. Doherty, New Jersey state president, Bank of America

"You have to be true to yourself, your values, and principles. Everybody—companies, individuals, leaders, and families—faces challenges. Being true to yourself, your values, and principles enables you to weather the storm and figure out the path forward to deal with the challenges and the extraordinary opportunities in front of you."

Leecia Eve, vice president state government affairs, NJ, NY, and CT Region, Verizon Communications

"Listen more than you speak. You can learn a lot by listening. You don't need to be the smartest person in the room, and you don't need to provide color commentary on everything."

Warren Geller, president and CEO, Englewood Hospital and Medical Center

"Leadership and innovation are synonymous. Leaders have to be on the edge of innovation and be thinking about changing their own model—building that better mousetrap, constantly. The status quo is not good enough in today's business environment."

Dennis Wilson, president and CEO, Delta Dental of New Jersey

"You can never over-communicate when it comes to change management. The simpler the message, the better—but you must continue to share where you are and where you are going with your people."

> Lata N. Reddy, vice president, Corporate Social
> Responsibility, and president, The Prudential
> Foundation at Prudential Financial

"Soft stuff matters. As a leader, you must spend time figuring out the kind of culture you need and how to get it. The culture of a company determines a lot."

> Josh S. Weston, honorary chairman, ADP, LLC

"Admit making mistakes. It may seem counterintuitive, because people don't want to accept the fact that leaders make mistakes, but we're all human and we do. The sooner we own those mistakes, say what we've learned from them, and commit to not making the same mistakes again, the better. As a leader, it doesn't make you look weaker. I think it makes you look stronger."

> Nancy Blattner, PhD, president, Caldwell University

"The biggest challenge for most leaders is around talent. It's a differentiator for all of us, so it's important to constantly ensure that you're bringing on the right people, you're retaining the right people, and you're making tough decisions around the people that perhaps should not be there."

> Linda Bowden, New Jersey regional president,
> PNC Bank

"I'm all about collaboration; not everyone is. The challenge is getting others to play in the sandbox. You can demand that they jump in, but they're not going to perform. They have to want to come in. Building the right environment so they want to be there is how you make it happen."

> Michele N. Siekerka, president and CEO,
> New Jersey Business and Industry Association

"Leaders act. Leaders go first. You cannot get caught up in explaining what should be done and what should not be done. Ultimately, the test of leadership is what is done. It's about action."

Chris Cuomo, anchor, *New Day*, CNN

"Leaders ignite something in people. They help people find their passion. They motivate them, and lift them up. Different than managers who light a fire under people, it's about lighting that passion and that fire within someone and helping them actualize *their* dreams as well."

Yesenia Madas, EdD, executive director, Center for Student Success, New Jersey Council of County Colleges

"Be transparent with your people, in the sense of what they are doing right and what they are doing wrong. And when you acknowledge that something is wrong, you must confront it as soon as possible rather than waiting. Once you wait, it just gets worse."

John H. Hajjar, MD, FACS, MBA, chairman and CEO, Sovereign Health System

"Never burn a bridge. You never know who you will end up working with again, so make sure you keep those relationships strong, even if you don't agree. Always be respectful and always be kind. The second lesson I've learned is remember who helped you get up because you will go back down."

Amy B. Mansue, president, Southern Region, RWJBarnabas Health

"Have a clear vision, build a great team, empower them, trust them, and work with them."

John Galandak, president, Commerce and Industry Association of New Jersey

"Spend time in the field with your team and employees. I've learned the more I listen and ask questions, the better I do, personally. Talk to people, listen to them, and try to solve problems."

James V. Fakult, president, Jersey Central Power & Light

"Take your emotions out of it. Not your passion, not your drive, but you have to learn to deal with your temperament."

The Rev. Al Sharpton, founder and president,
National Action Network

"One, build great teams. Two, get your emotions out of the way and, instead, make sure that you stay on point for what the mission is by being adaptable. And three, humility."

Marjorie A. Perry, president and CEO, MZM Construction
& Management Company

"Listen to people. Find out what their problems are. Find out what they need, and find a way to get it to them."

Thomas A. Bracken, president and CEO,
New Jersey Chamber of Commerce

"When you're in a confrontation with someone and something has happened that you're not crazy about, always ask before you accuse. Ask a question and put the other person in the position where they can explain themselves."

Ken Schlager, editor, *New Jersey Monthly*

"Be ready to serve. A lot of people confuse leadership with a title or some type of position, but that's not what leadership is. You have to be with your team in the midst of the vision that you're trying to carry out and be the first one ready to get your hands dirty."

Evelyn Mejil, executive director and CEO,
Senator Wynona Lipman Child Advocacy Center

"Be generous and consistent."

Steven Kern, director and CEO, Newark Museum

"Listen to others. You can't just assume that you have all the answers. Ask for feedback and connect with people on a human level."

Patricia Stark, communications coach,
anchor, Fox News Channel

"You must have a set of convictions you believe in, but more importantly, you need to realize that often you're wrong and you should listen carefully to what the people around you have to say. Listening and agreeing is not always the same thing, but you have to be able to listen, change, and adapt."

Christopher Cerf, superintendent,
Newark Public Schools, New Jersey

"Treat people with integrity, keep your promises, and make sure everyone understands we're all in this together."

Roger Michaud, senior vice president,
Franklin Templeton Investments

"Don't be afraid to speak your mind respectfully and don't be afraid to fail. Great leaders have to be decisive, and when you're decisive, sometimes you make the wrong decision. But you always need to be ready to learn from that decision, pick yourself back up, and move on."

Elizabeth A. Ryan, Esq., president and CEO,
New Jersey Hospital Association

"Trust your gut and go with your first instinct, because 99 percent of the time it's right."

Andrew Duke, president and owner, Metrographics

"Don't ask a team member to do something or to take something on that you yourself are unwilling to do. As a leader, don't have an ego. Your team should feel that they could ask of you what you ask of them."

Carlos A. Medina, Esq., chairman, Statewide Hispanic
Chamber of Commerce of New Jersey

"Listen carefully to what people are saying to you so that you appreciate the nuances of what they're trying to present. Your understanding of a situation can improve dramatically."

Daniel Hart, professor of childhood studies
and psychology, Rutgers University

"Find someone who is doing something you're doing and is really successful at it. Find their number, call them, and ask them for advice. Usually they will help you."

Linda Wellbrock, founder and CEO, Leading Women
Entrepreneurs & Business Owners

"You need to have the passion and the energy to wake up every day and move through every obstacle. You must believe in your mission to your core, because when you do, it gets you up in the morning and gets you over that fence."

Ron Beit, founding partner and CEO,
RBH Group, LLC

"Leadership is about knowing how to manage others and how to bring leaders out of your team. Building other leaders is what I'm most proud of."

Heather Thomson, founder
and CCO, Yummie

"Listen to the people around you, because sometimes they have better ideas than you have. Don't be insecure. Lead by example but also recognize you can lead by following."

Vinnie Favale, vice president of CBS Late Night Programming and co-creator of the musical *Hereafter*

"The challenge is getting everyone in your organization to understand what you're trying to do, why you're trying to do it, and then enlist their support in getting there."

Jack Miller, president and CEO, Solix, Inc.

"When the stakes are high the senior person has to make the decision, but it is prudent and smart to listen to absolutely everybody. While you may have been doing things one way for years, someone simply asking 'Why?' can raise a very good question that may just make you improve your process."

Joseph Maguire, vice admiral, United States Navy (Ret.); president and CEO, Special Operations Warrior Foundation

"You don't have to take credit for everything. It's important to give credit to your coworkers."

Noreen Springstead, executive director, WhyHunger

"The reality is you have to bring people along with you. You can't push them, you can't pull them. You have to convince them that what you have is the right thing. Eventually, that helps them work harder for you."

Ras J. Baraka, mayor, Newark, New Jersey

"As a leader, you have to believe in what you're doing if you expect others to follow you. Especially when you're a teacher, asking children to follow you is an awesome responsibility. My students are prepared to follow me, so I better be clear and sure of where I'm leading them."

Anne McCormick, chemistry teacher,
Jackson Memorial High School, New Jersey

"Be honest and take care of your people. Get people on your side and make them part of the team. Anyone who has run a big organization knows that people make the difference."

Bernard Schwartz, author, *Just Say Yes*

"Leadership is about understanding what makes your operation go. You have to get the right people on the bus to get the job done."

Dana L. Redd, mayor, Camden, New Jersey

"Leverage your contacts, relationships, network, and community in positive ways. I don't mean using people. I mean being in circles where what you do can be beneficial to others, where you can demonstrate your leadership skills, and where you can learn from other leaders."

Lynnette Khalfani-Cox, personal finance expert,
TheMoneyCoach.net LLC

2

Great Leaders Sometimes "Piss People Off"

There are so many theories and philosophies of what makes a great leader. I have talked to leaders of all stripes about their challenges and frustrations, as well as their secrets of success. But every once in a while, you come across a leadership lesson that is irrefutable, and interestingly it was told to me in a public television interview with General Colin Powell about fifteen years ago. At the time, I asked General Powell about the essence of leadership, and he said, "Being a great leader means sometimes pissing people off." What? I'll never forget those words. They have come back to me again and again in my executive coaching and leadership seminars as well as in my own role as a leader.

Recently, I was talking with a hospital executive about the challenges of leadership. I happened to mention the Colin Powell quote to him, and he said, "That's funny, I have that same quote hanging right in my office." When we walked into his office, there it was. General Powell's "Leadership Primer," in which he offered eighteen leadership lessons. Lesson 1: "Being responsible sometimes means pissing people off." So, Powell didn't just flippantly tell me this in a public television interview, he wrote it in his book on leadership, and he practices it as well.

Powell's point is insightful and profound. Too many of us, in leadership positions, are too concerned with wanting people to like us and every decision we make. We want everyone to accept and like the way we handle different situations, even if it requires direct, candid, and hard-to-hear feedback or criticism. That is simply not always possible or sometimes preferable. Says Powell, "Trying to get everyone to like you is a sign of mediocrity: you'll avoid the tough decisions, you'll avoid confronting the people who need to be confronted, and you'll avoid offering differential rewards based on differential performance because some people might get upset."

Powell is right. The irony is that when we don't make the tough choices as leaders because we want to be nice to everyone all the time or treat them equally, regardless of their performance, we guarantee mediocrity. The fact is, being a great leader requires that sometimes you will make decisions that make people on your team unhappy or pissed off. You may need to say something directly, without mincing words, that someone is performing under par or is behaving unacceptably: "Jim, we need to talk specifically about how you are not getting the job done and we need to come up with a plan to turn it around quickly. If not, it is not going to be good for you or for our team." Your goal is not to threaten Jim but rather to tell him exactly where things stand and what is expected moving forward.

When you talk with Jim in such a fashion, he is not going to walk out of your office singing your praises. In fact, there is a good chance he goes into his office and texts or calls his wife to tell her what a jerk you are: "Do you believe the nerve of this guy? How dare he talk to me this way after all the years I've given to this place? I am so peeved." I've seen this kind of reaction in others to this kind of direct leadership approach—haven't you?

But what would happen if you didn't have that conversation with Jim, knowing that his performance had been subpar for so long? What if you chose to deal with the situation by doing nothing and just hoping things got better? A huge leadership lesson to remember: Hope is not a plan, particularly for a good leader. I'm not advocating that you "piss people off" just for the sake of it or because you can. That's just arrogant and contentious. Being respectful and courteous is a priority for any leader. However, occasionally "pissing people off" goes with the territory if you are the kind of leader that deals directly and honestly with your people and situations that must be confronted. The alternative is unacceptable; the outcome of such a passive approach will be much worse for you and for your team.

The Price of Not Confronting: The Case of Paul

Paul is a bank manager in his mid-thirties, who is well liked, hardworking, and respected in his company. Yet, recently, Paul's CEO suggested some executive coaching as a way to help him take his skills to the next level.

A little background. While no one questions Paul's willingness to work hard and be a team player, he is reluctant to "step up," as his boss says. In my capacity as the executive coach for this bank, the boss explains that Paul runs meetings that ramble and are unfocused. "He is such a nice guy. He often seems reluctant to cut people off when they are on a tangent." He also says that when Paul's team fails to come to any consensus or decision, he tends to put off that same agenda item until the next meeting. Over time, these less-than-stellar leadership skills have hurt Paul's career advancement.

During a recent coaching session, I asked Paul about these issues. His response was revealing. "I am really uncomfortable confronting people. It is not my style to be in someone's face and I don't like it when people do it to me." As the session continued, it became clear that Paul saw "confrontation" as exclusively a negative thing. Along with so many other professionals, Paul saw confrontation as a form of aggression, as something that makes people uncomfortable. He saw confrontation as a battle, a contest, a war fought by combatants who will either win or lose. He wanted no part of it.

Clearly, confrontation can be and sometimes is many of these things. But there is another way to look at "confrontational leadership" as an opportunity to deal with an ongoing problem or challenge head-on. Not confronting it would mean missing a big opportunity. How many of us have long-simmering, below-the-surface feuds with people we need to get along with? It could be at work or in your personal life. Or well before a feud, there might be just a misunderstanding or incident at work or at home that is eating at you, affecting your interaction with a certain person or persons and undermining productivity and the overall work or home environment. Leadership lesson: In these situations, you *must* artfully confront things head-on. The alternative is not a viable option. Things rarely get better on their own—or over time.

Consider Paul, our bank manager, who needs to say to his colleagues who refuse to reach a decision on a crucial business matter: "Let's be clear: by not coming to a decision on X we stand to lose a lot of revenue. If our team is unwilling or unable to decide, I will do it because the alternative will produce an unacceptable outcome."

When Paul was presented with this more direct leadership approach in our coaching session, he said, "I can do that! But that's not being confrontational." Yes it is! It is confronting your colleagues (or others) with your candid view of a situation. It's confronting by framing the consequences of our action or inaction by stating how you see things. Confrontation in this form is an essential leadership tool.

The Lesson of Artful Confrontation

On a personal level, I encourage you to confront anyone with whom you have longstanding issues or concerns that are truly bothering you. Not the "small stuff" of little consequence, as the late author Richard Carlson advised us not to "sweat" in his groundbreaking series of books *Don't Sweat the Small Stuff.* Why not tell your wife or husband or someone close to you, "When I do something extra special for you, and you don't even acknowledge it or say thanks, it makes me feel really lousy." No malice. No animosity. No rancor or battle to fight. Just your honest assessment about something that matters—from the heart. That's right, confronting the issue. The situation. There is no guarantee that you will get the reaction you want or need, but at least it is better than ruminating about it, complaining to others, or acting out in anger and frustration without ever saying what is causing it. As I said, the alternative to ignoring or ducking the situation only makes things worse and gets you more frustrated and angry.

Yes, this more artful "confrontational leadership" approach has the potential to make folks on the receiving end uncomfortable or even "pissed off," but it also dramatically increases the odds of your making some progress in an unacceptable situation. It's worth the risk. Trust me.

3

You Can't Lead Others Until
You Learn to Lead Yourself

Losing it. Blowing your cool. Acting like a jerk in public. Playing the victim. Overreacting. Pouting, complaining, yelling. You get the picture. We've all been there. I know I have, way more often than I'd like to admit—not only in my personal life, but in my position as a leader. And every time it happens, nothing good comes from it, and I wonder why it ever happened in the first place.

For years, I was convinced that the only way to lead an organization was to take the "broken-windows theory" (made popular by Rudy Giuliani and the New York City police department in the 1990s) and use that as my bible. Simply put, the broken-windows theory postulates that as soon as a window is broken, as soon as the smallest mistake occurs, the organization's leader must follow a zero-tolerance approach and philosophy. Not following this approach sends the wrong message to everyone—that such "small" mistakes are no big deal, and then bigger ones are likely to follow. While this leadership philosophy may work when it comes to crime in America's biggest and most metropolitan cities, in a small organization like mine, it has sometimes resulted in simply coming down much too hard and for too long on team members. Not only when things went wrong, but also when things just didn't turn out right—even if it was nobody's fault.

Sometimes, it would cause me to stop listening and be resistant to feedback. I would consider any explanation to be an excuse. Sure, we have high standards for the work we do, and we have a great track record, but there was a lot of unnecessary "collateral damage" in the process. The problem is that collateral damage involves real people and their emotions and feelings. We're not talking about empty buildings or some broken windows. Please don't confuse this with the need to "piss people off" as a leader when dealing with legitimate performance issues or making tough staff decisions by engaging in artful confrontation, a lesson offered by General Colin Powell, which I talk about in chapter 2.

I don't want to be overly dramatic or engage in "armchair psychiatry," but I am pretty sure I know where a lot of this came from. For years, I saw my father take this approach as a leader and implement it big-time—kind of like "broken windows" on steroids. I often used to think that compared with my father's, my leadership approach was more like Gandhi's. That would be my rationalization, my attempt at explaining I really wasn't that tough and difficult. But the fact is, looking back, I realize now that I wasn't leading myself and my emotions in the way I should have been. I was simply "losing it" too often, all in the name of keeping high standards. Over time, with lots of introspection and some great advice from others, I've found that you can maintain very high standards for performance and execution but go about it in a very different way. It is probably one of the best leadership lessons I've ever learned; but as I said, sometimes I wish it hadn't taken me so long to figure this out. That's why, later in this chapter, I share my journey with you—warts and all—not holding anything back.

What we may not realize is that as leaders, when we "lose it" we send many powerful messages and do significant damage. A commonly cited study has found that 55 percent of all human interaction is based on body language, while 38 percent is based on vocal inflection and tone. Our actual words equal 7 percent of the human relations game.[1] For leaders, knowing this is extremely important. Acting on it is essential.

One of the places where body language, as well as our vocal tone and inflection, speaks volumes is on the golf course. As you read this book, it will become clear that I have come to the conclusion that the game of golf is in many ways a metaphor for the challenges of leadership and for life. It can happen in any arena, including the workplace. In many ways, golf is like the game of life. Stuff happens and much of it is unexpected and unwelcome. It's what you do with it that matters. Consider the following examples of losing it:

- You miss a three-foot putt that you know you should make. You immediately drop your putter (or throw it) and loudly blurt out, "@#$%! I hate this game! Why did I even play today?"
- You hit what you think is a perfect shot. As the ball is heading directly to the green, it takes a bad bounce into the sand trap. You start complaining about the unfairness of it all. Shaking your head, you bellow, "You've got to be kidding me! That was a great shot! What kind of bounce was that? When will I catch a break?" The other golfers (trying to play their own game) are thinking to themselves, "What a jerk. Does he think he's the only one who gets a bad break?"
- You are on the tee, where it's supposed to be quiet. But as usual, that's not the case because others are playing. Just as you are about to hit the ball, you hear the sound of another golfer. You hit the ball into the woods. Oh no, you're going to lose it again! "That's it!" you declare, as you take the driver and hit it into the ground—really hard—causing the shaft of the driver to crack. Head down, you mumble to yourself. Just then, another golfer asks you if you know where *his* driver is. Apparently, the guy put his driver into your golf bag, which you used mistakenly and then broke.

I share these golf stories because I've witnessed them firsthand, and in some cases, I was the offending party and I'm not proud of it. But these anecdotes do say a lot about us as people and as leaders of ourselves. And as I said, I am not proud of the times I've lost it, and clearly, even though leadership is my business, I still have a lot of work to do in this area. No matter what we *say*, it's often how we *act* that sends the most powerful messages to others. Losing it, letting your temper get the best of you, and blaming other people or things for your own mistakes is a no-win proposition. It gets you more frustrated, and it doesn't help your relationships with others.

Over the years, I've worked hard to manage my emotions or, put another way, handle myself differently in a variety of situations, at work as a leader and a teammate as well as in my personal life. I am better, but I still have a long way to go. One of the keys to leading yourself, when the potential of being overly emotional exists, is to gain a better sense of perspective. Yet, this is sometimes really hard to do on your own. For me, the biggest lessons have come from reading and learning from others who seem a lot smarter or wiser than me in this area.

One of the biggest influences on me has been the work of Richard Carlson and his groundbreaking series, *Don't Sweat the Small Stuff*. I remember reading a particular chapter that really struck me, which I must have reread 100 times by now. The chapter is called, "Will It Matter a Year from Now?" In the chapter, Carlson who died before he even turned fifty, leaving a wife and young children behind and a massive cadre of fans and supporters, talks about how angry and overly emotional we sometimes get about the "little things" that often happen in the world of business or in our everyday lives. He says that asking ourselves whether what has happened will matter all that much a year from now is a great way to put things in perspective before we respond and react to a particular situation.[2] This advice has definitely not kept me from getting peeved or miffed over certain situations or things that go wrong or not my way, but it has made a huge difference in how often it happens and the duration and intensity of these emotional blips.

Governor Chris Christie's "It's Who I Am" Leadership Style

Another leader who has influenced my perspective on the topic of leading oneself is New Jersey governor Chris Christie, whom I sat down with for a special interview for public television in December 2014. During this interview, one of the many I have done with the governor, we discussed a range of important issues, from New Jersey's post–Superstorm Sandy recovery to the governor's presidential aspirations. As is often the case when it comes to Governor Christie, our conversation also touched upon how his demeanor and what others perceive to be an aggressive leadership style has impacted his public life and how it may in fact have played a role at the time in the prospects of his running for the presidency.

In many ways, Christie's blunt, "tell it like it is" demeanor has been his calling card. Yet, there are some who have questioned the governor's aggressive leadership style and the fact that there have been times when he has confronted situations and certain people with language and tone that raise questions about his temperament. With this in mind, I asked Governor Christie if he had any intention of doing anything to tone down, tweak, or alter his demeanor as he considered a potential presidential run. In our public television interview he responded simply, "No, why would I? It's who I am. If people want somebody different, then if I ever ran for president, then they would vote for somebody different, but I don't intend to become a phony to win an election." In response, I pressed, "All of us try to tweak, modify, or change wherever we think we can be better. Are there times where you say to yourself, 'You know what, maybe there was a different way to handle that?' Not that you change your personality or become a different person." I was referring to the moment in October 2014 when Christie told a protester in the audience of a Belmar, New Jersey, press conference to "*Sit down and shut up*" for continuing to interrupt his speech. The governor went on to explain that in the ninety seconds leading up to that moment (which has gone viral in the media), he in fact let the guy yell, block the cameras with his signs, speak over him, get booed by the crowd, and yet, said Christie, "I said nothing except continue to try to give my speech. When I finally got to the point where people were booing, people were upset, we needed to move on, and this person was making a rude spectacle of himself, I said, 'I'm happy to talk to you alone later but, until then, sit down and shut up.' I don't regret that for one second and I wouldn't change that part of myself."

Governor Christie also recalled his interview with NBC's Matt Lauer of the *Today Show* during which he was asked a similar question regarding his demeanor. Lauer asked, "Do you have to control yourself more when you run for president?" According to Christie, he responded, "What makes you think that I wasn't under control? What makes you think that wasn't exactly what I wanted to do? While it might not be what you would do, it was what I would do." Christie went on to explain to me on public television, "You know what I think the most important thing is when you're deciding to vote for someone? Do you know them? Who are they? Are they trying to fool you or are they giving you who they are? Nobody thinks I'm trying to fool them."

Governor Christie reinforced his commitment to this leadership approach in the inaugural video of his 2016 presidential campaign titled, "Telling It Like It Is," which was released in June 2015. In the two-minute video, Christie is shown explaining to a town hall crowd why he's the blunt politician many know him for. In it, he describes what he calls his "moral compass" and tells a story about a lesson he learned from his mother to never hold back feelings in a trusting relationship. "When people wonder why I do the things I do, that moment affirmed for me—forever—that I'm going to be this way," Christie says. "I know if my mom were still alive she would say to me, 'I taught you that in a trusting relationship you don't hold anything back, and if you're going to run for president of the United States and you're going to ask these people for their vote, that is the single most trusting thing they can do as a citizen is to give you their support, so you better tell them exactly what you're thinking and exactly what you're feeling.'"

Ultimately, Chris Christie's presidential campaign ended after the New Hampshire primary. The reasons for this are complex and multifaceted. Beyond presidential politics, there is an important leadership lesson to be learned. Being honest, establishing trust, and, yes, making sure people know you are going to "tell it like it is" are all important parts of being a leader. Yet, leaders who do these things must also be committed to controlling their emotions and ultimately controlling themselves, because when times are tough or things don't go exactly as planned it becomes all the more difficult to keep their emotions from getting the best of them.

Christie argues he is very much in control of himself, and only he knows for sure if that's true. While I respect the governor greatly and also consider him a friend, he and I differ on the definition of "being a phony" as trying to change or improve the way a leader handles certain situations over time. I don't think the governor would be a phony at all if he tempered his response and emotional reaction to certain situations. In fact, I think he's done that strategically; though I'm convinced that he believes articulating or saying this publicly—to me or to anyone in the media—is a sign of weakness. During our public television interview, he went as far as to say, "What you'll do and what others would do with that piece of tape is you'll take a small piece of whatever I say and then you will use that to say, 'See, Christie said he will change.'" The governor and I disagree. I see it as a plus. I see it as strength. But then again, reasonable people can disagree, and I don't expect Governor Christie to change his opinion or his approach to leadership based on what I'm saying anytime soon. That's what makes him so unique, as well as the other leaders featured in this book. That's also what makes leadership such a fascinating topic.

The Demeanor and Leadership Connection

Switching gears, while I talk about Governor Christie's demeanor, which has been a great part of his story as New Jersey's chief executive, I must be candid and admit that my changing perspective on this entire question of demeanor has probably come a little too late. As I said earlier in this chapter, over the years, I have found myself losing it over things that went wrong, or not the way I would have liked, around professional colleagues and people who work on my team, which has caused me to react in a way that was simply unacceptable by any leadership standard. Over time, I wound up losing some good people on our team, and I am convinced that no matter what they said as to why they left, my demeanor as a leader in certain circumstances contributed to their decision to leave.

In fact, in arguably the most significant professional relationship I've ever had, this inability or lack of willingness to manage myself as a leader and avoid losing it has contributed to the potential loss of my number-one person. My longtime colleague, Mary Gamba, came to me about a year before this book had to go to press and expressed a desire to pursue other professional options. Such decisions are complex and multifaceted, and for Mary, a lot of it was personal on many levels, having to do with things that she wanted to accomplish in her professional life.

However, I am convinced that part of the equation for Mary had to do with the times over the years when my response and reaction to certain situations and circumstances when things didn't go swimmingly or the way I wanted them to go were simply inappropriate. I blamed too much, overreacted, wouldn't let it go, lost my cool, and just didn't manage myself and my emotions the way a good leader should. Ultimately, after a series of extensive and meaningful conversations in which Mary "renegotiated her contract," she agreed to stay. But it was in these conversations that Mary also candidly shared her frustrations with my handling of certain situations and came clean that while she did want to pursue other interests, my less-than-glowing demeanor at times definitely contributed to her decision to consider walking away.

And a year later, while I am sure there are things she wants to accomplish professionally and personally that in some cases are beyond my control, we are a better team than ever. Mary has gone out of her way to tell me how much more satisfied and fulfilled she has felt over the past year, and how committed she is to the work she is doing (a flexible work schedule and a significant bonus may have helped). When I asked her why, she shared, "I have an increased passion and enthusiasm just knowing that when things go wrong, and they will go wrong, that you now make a conscious effort to be more solution-oriented, rather than looking to assign blame. It is clear that you have made a commitment to managing your emotions, and your more positive attitude has made a difference in not only our relationship but also the morale of the entire team."

You see, the fear of God was put into this particular leader, who realized that there are serious consequences when you fail to truly lead yourself and the emotions that go with it, because of the impact it has on those whom you interact with professionally and personally.

It's not that I wasn't prepared to move on professionally without Mary; it's that I wanted to do what I could to improve myself as a leader by managing myself and my emotions more effectively. I also recognized the potential impact my "losing it" had, not only on our relationships, but on the productivity of our team and organization. By any reasonable standard, the result has been extremely successful. But it's a constantly evolving dynamic process, and the danger of slipping back into old, not-so-healthy leadership habits is always a risk.

The bottom line here is that leaders have no right to expect others to have a positive attitude, to deal with difficult circumstances or to basically work in a collegial fashion if they too often "lose it" and do not lead themselves and their emotions with a sense of calm and a "we're all in this together" approach.

4

In Leadership (and in Life), Attitude Is Everything

Leaders' attitudes affect and can infect all those around them as well as their organization's effectiveness. Their attitudes pervade the meetings they lead, the way they deal with their people when problems occur, how they negotiate challenging situations, and how they engage team members about how they're going to face the difficult road ahead. Leaders with a negative, defeatist attitude often wind up de-motivating the people on their team. Some of them say they are just being realistic or "telling it like it is." While I have no problem with stating how difficult the problem or challenge may be, if the people on your team are convinced that *you* are convinced failure is inevitable, how could you think it wouldn't affect their performance?

People often say our attitude is a direct byproduct of the circumstances we find ourselves in. It's understandable to see the world that way, and frankly, for much of the time, that's the way I see things. But when a video was sent to me about Nick Vujicic, a man who was born with no arms and no legs and is now one of the most powerful and effective motivational speakers in the country and has been featured on *60 Minutes*, I was forced to step back, check myself, and ask, "What exactly are you complaining about?" In fact, truly great leaders—more often than not—actually choose their attitude. That's right, they choose it. They make a conscious decision, no matter what the circumstance or situation, to say the following: "Clearly the situation stinks and I'd rather have it not be this way . . . but since I can't change all that, I might as well figure out how to make the best of it because the alternative will clearly be worse."

While writing this book, I've looked back at some of the work of the late Dr. Richard Carlson, the author of the mega-selling book series, *Don't Sweat the Small Stuff*, which I mention in several chapters. Carlson's work has had a great impact on me over the years, and I find myself going back to his writings at especially challenging times for me both professionally and personally. Carlson also wrote a less well known book called *You Can Be Happy No Matter What*, in which he talked about the way most of us try to look at and solve problems by obsessing over trying to change our circumstances.

Carlson's view on problems was very different. Carlson argued that "circumstances are always neutral."[1] What he meant by this is that of course you want your boss to be more understanding, you want that raise, and you wish that your partner or professional colleague were less argumentative. We want to be healthy all the time.

But ask yourself how often you've actually been able to change someone else's behavior or a particular circumstance. It is great when we can, and there is nothing wrong with our trying to achieve this, but things get dicey when we convince ourselves that all circumstances are within our ability to control, if not change. Further, we think that if we are fortunate enough to change a situation, everything will be fine.

For that guy who complains about not getting a raise, but finally *does* get it, look what happens just a few months after. He is complaining about something else, like "Why does Jim get the corner office with the big window and I am stuck in this tiny room facing this stupid wall?" Carlson argued, quite compellingly, that sometimes it is a lot more effective to focus on changing our mood and how we choose to look at a situation as opposed to obsessing over changing our circumstances. This view can have a direct effect on how we deal with the challenges and obstacles we face as well as our overall approach to leadership.

Have you ever noticed that when you are in a bad or down mood, virtually everything bothers you—people you live and work with, the job itself (if you are lucky enough to have a job these days), the weather, traffic, children, and whatever else impacts your life? But the next day, or maybe even just a few hours later, those same circumstances don't seem exactly the same.

As I am an avid golfer, this is something that has always amazed me about the game. Sometimes, after playing terribly for the first few holes and being convinced it is going to be a long, terrible slog through eighteen holes, my regular golfing partners Nick Matarazzo and Andy Duke will remind me that "There's a lot of golf left to play" or "It's early, Steve . . . relax." Sure enough, more often than not, things will turn around and I'll have a string of pars or even a few birdies. All after being convinced none of this was possible. My friends Nick and Andy have taught me this valuable golf lesson, which translates to both leadership and life. In turn, I've used it with others on the golf course who are having a few tough holes and are turning negative, convinced that things can't turn around. Attitude is a funny thing. Believing things can get better, or, in fact, will get better, has a direct impact on the way you perform. The converse is true as well. I've seen it and lived it on the golf course and have also experienced it in the workplace and in life. If you think about it, you'll acknowledge how true this really is.

Further, when you are in a better and healthier frame of mind, we often see more creative options, alternatives, and potential solutions to the nagging problems we face every day, even the big ones. So, doesn't it make more sense to focus on trying to change—or at least tweak—our mood and try to be more consistently upbeat than it does to engage in a futile exercise of changing everyone and everything around us or wishing things were different?

Your attitude is *your* choice. Only *you* can decide whether to see that glass as half full or half empty. When I'm on my game, I choose to see it as half full, but when I'm not, it makes things a lot worse. Plus, I wind up getting more frustrated and acting like a victim—not a leader.

When leaders choose to have a positive attitude in this way, they have the ability to motivate and inspire those around them to greatness and get through the most trying and challenging times. They can positively influence the energy of the team and the psyche of each team member. Consider three very special people who faced very difficult and, in fact, devastating circumstances, yet chose to rise above it and made not only the best of their situation but ultimately turned it into a positive. That is the essence of leadership—taking whatever situation or circumstance you are presented with and turning it around. Making lemonade out of lemons. This sounds like such a cliché but it's the truth. Read on and you'll see what I mean.

Eric LeGrand Focuses on What He *Can* Do— A Lesson for All of Us

I am writing this chapter in the winter during one of the countless snowstorms that has hit us over the past weeks. It's funny how people say the weather affects your attitude. I'm convinced this is true, because I've been cranky, short, and irritated by the little things. Simply, I'm not at my best and not a lot of fun to be around. Can you relate? Winter is funny that way. So is snow and bad weather overall. Yet, there is a much bigger picture for some people who have overcome a lot more than a little snow.

Consider the case of Eric LeGrand, the former Rutgers University football standout, who was featured in the *Star-Ledger* a while back by my former *Star-Ledger* colleague Steve Politi—a celebrated sports columnist. As many people know, LeGrand was paralyzed after a devastating hit on the football field on October 16, 2010. For many, it's inconceivable that in the blink of an eye, a strapping, strong, fit, and extremely young athlete would go from the top of his game to being paralyzed in a wheelchair.

But here's the thing about attitude. It can help you do things that otherwise seem improbable, if not impossible. Not only is Eric LeGrand consistently ahead of his doctors' expectations, he has become an inspirational leader, not just on the Rutgers campus, but for so many who have suffered a debilitating injury and are facing daunting odds. In virtually every picture of LeGrand, he has a huge smile on his face, which is only matched by the upbeat and inspiring words that come out of his mouth. Amazingly, he told Politi, "I'm thankful for what I have now, but you don't settle for it. You have to keep looking forward."[2]

So while the rest of us wait for better weather to change our mood, Eric LeGrand apparently decided that he was going to change his attitude from the inside out. He decided what his future holds.

Months after he was paralyzed, LeGrand said, "I always wanted to be a sportscaster. . . . My dream was to play in the NFL, but after that, it's to be a sportscaster. I'll probably focus on that after I graduate college."[3] (He wound up as part of the Rutgers radio broadcast.) He also talked about the possibility of coaching. When LeGrand got out of Kessler Institute for Rehabilitation in West Orange, New Jersey, at the end of March 2011, he began a whirlwind of activity, inspiring others not just through his words but through his actions and, again, his attitude. He became a leader by seizing the moment and making the most of it.

LeGrand has continued to speak to individuals facing serious injuries and has shown them what is possible through hard work, dedication, and an incredibly positive attitude. While many of us allow negative communication to impact our lives, he says, "I can honestly say I don't talk to the doctors—my family handles them."[4] The reason is that very often, those doctors tell him what he *can't* do, while LeGrand wants to focus on what he *can* do. Again, this attitude directly impacts his approach to life and the challenges he faces.

In the first year after his devastating injury, LeGrand said that he's only cried four or five times. Ultimately, he says, "I never get angry. . . . There's no reason to get angry. I know, in time, it's going to happen. I was never a patient person. I'm learning through this that I have to be patient, and it will all come back." Until then, he said, "I'm living life the best way I can."[5]

What else can anyone ask for? Living life the best you can. Making the most of what you have. Focusing on what you *can* do. What a powerful lesson in leadership and life. Eric LeGrand proves it every day. To say he is a role model for the rest of us is a massive understatement. To say he is a hero seems more like it.

We Can't Change What Cards We Are Dealt, but We Can Choose How We Play Them

Every once in a while, you meet someone who helps put things in perspective by dealing with adversity in a positive, upbeat, and inspirational manner—simply put, a leader who inspires with her optimistic attitude in spite of the odds. Meet Julia Spencer. You probably don't know her name, but Spencer's book, *Looking through a Keyhole*, is one you should go out and buy.[6]

I had Julia Spencer in the studio for a public television interview a few years ago, and even though I had read about her, actually meeting her was even more powerful. She was seventy-eight years young at the time and a yoga instructor, which is impressive in and of itself. But consider the fact that at age fifty, she began to lose her eyesight because of a degenerative genetic disease called retinitis pigmentosa. Her sister suffers from it and is totally blind. Other relatives also have it.

As Spencer walked in to the studio with her seeing-eye dog, Irene, she was bright and cheery, with a smile on her face. When I finally shook her hand, she wanted me to know that while she couldn't see my body or most of my face, she could see my eyes. She has no peripheral vision, but it seems to me that what Julia actually sees is a lot more than the rest of us.

We all have friends and business associates who consistently whine and complain in a negative and depressing fashion. They play the victim, saying things like: "Why did I even go into this stupid profession? I should have been a ———." Or, "Why does Bob make that kind of money? I should have that job." They are whiners and complainers. I, too, throw a pity party for myself more often than I'd like, but what continues to strike me is that the attitude we choose to have, regardless of our circumstances, dictates the way we deal with the situation and engage with others.

Julia Spencer has decided to have a positive attitude, and she lives her life reflecting it every day. Here's just a sampling of some of the things she told me during our conversation:

"I use yoga to find peace. Peace is internal, not external."

"Whenever I have bad times in my life, I write."

"I went to New York City by myself to prove that I was independent. My husband wasn't happy about it; however, I learned that you can be independent and still ask for help."

"Don't pity anyone, because people who are totally blind live meaningful and fulfilling lives."

So here's the deal. As you are reading this, ask yourself, "What's my attitude and how can I improve it?" As the late Randy Pausch (who wrote the terrific book *The Last Lecture*) said, "We can't change what cards we're dealt, but we can choose how we play them." That's the way Spencer lives her life. Think about it. At age seventy-eight, she was a yoga instructor. At eighty-two, she still is! She wrote a book to inspire others. While others say things like "I ought to write a book," Julia Spencer actually did it. While some people talk about life's challenges and complain, Julia decided that she will live her life with a positive attitude, and she has become a truly inspirational leader in the process. She inspires the rest of us to take a closer look at ourselves and the way we see the world. If Spencer has accomplished all of this, being eighty-two years old and blind, I can't imagine what she'll do at ninety.

A Lesson in Leadership from the Boston Marathon: Turning Tragedy into Something Special

What happened in the 2014 Boston Marathon was a tragedy on so many levels. The idea that two very sick and hateful brothers would plant and detonate bombs to ensure the maximum amount of human destruction at such a positive event is hard to comprehend. Lives were lost. Limbs and families were torn apart. The survivors of the Boston Marathon bombing continue to suffer the effects of that day. Those of us who have been at so many public functions and events should remind ourselves every day to say, "There but for the grace of God go I." It could have happened to any of us, but it happened to those people.

As the brave victims in Boston were recovering and dealing with their devastating injuries, I, like millions of other Americans, found myself losing perspective on the "small stuff." Simply put, a long-time sponsor of our public television series called to say the company was experiencing some unexpected financial troubles and had to pull its sponsorship. In the following hours and days, I had to think through the implications of losing one major sponsor. My game was thrown off. It took me longer than it should have to realize that I had to quickly shift gears and identify new alternatives. That's what good leaders do, right?

Instead, I found myself complaining to those around me, including my staff and family. "I don't get it. It's not fair. A committed sponsor of over ten years pulls out? How can we plan our operation this way?" My complaining continued: "By the way, why do I have to be the one to raise all this money anyway?" I kept talking about fairness—or my convoluted definition of it. It's funny. Putting the words "fair" and "business" in the same sentence is like putting the words "fair" and "life" in the same sentence or, better yet, "fair" and "leadership" in the same sentence.

Let me put things in perspective and introduce you to Adrianne Haslet-Davis, who was watching the Boston Marathon with her husband when the bomb went off about five feet away from her. Haslet-Davis is a passionate ballroom dancer who happened to be at the wrong place at the wrong time, and her foot was blown off. She was also interviewed by the *Boston Herald* and told them that while at times she was angry and wondered why this happened, she realized you have to be selfish about the things that matter the most. Said Haslet-Davis, "My husband. The job I love.

Dancing is my life. Yeah, having my foot blown off, that really sucks. But I can't wallow in woe is me . . . I'll dance again. And next year, though I've never been a runner, yes, I plan to run the marathon."[7]

Adrianne Haslet-Davis made a choice. She couldn't change the past. She could have asked, as many others probably would have, "Why me?" How many of us do that over so much less? Life is unfair, and so is leadership. As I watched Haslet-Davis and the countless other Boston heroes who lost limbs but were determined to make the most of what they had left, I asked myself this question: "If *they* could do it, what about the rest of us?" For me, just thinking about people like Haslet-Davis serves as a reminder that the next time something inevitably goes wrong, instead of asking "Why me?" the better question is "Why not me?" And, more importantly, now that it's happened, "What are you going to do about it to make things better?"

All Haslet-Davis was doing was standing at the Boston Marathon. A bomb went off. But she didn't let this stop her from having hope. In fact, at the 2015 Boston Marathon, she showcased her determination and did so in a flowing ball gown as she danced the foxtrot across the race finish line. So why should our challenges and obstacles stop us? The truth is, they are not what stops us. *We* are what stops us. *I* am what stops me when I overreact to the "small stuff," be it as a player on the golf course or as a leader responsible for a significant media production company or anyone of you reading this book who are in a leadership position responsible for other people as well as the bottom line. Simply put, we have a choice. If that's not a lesson in leadership, I don't know what is.

Ultimately, as I say in chapter 3 you can't lead others until you *choose* to lead yourself. But more importantly, you have to continually choose your attitude. That's what the inspirational individuals discussed in this chapter—Eric LeGrand, Julia Spencer, and Adrianne Haslet-Davis—did, along with countless others who face daunting challenges and sometimes terrible tragedy but choose, not to give up or give in, but rather to live life and make the most of it.

Staying Positive, Even When the Answer Is "No"

One of the challenges that many leaders face is how to handle rejection, or simply how to react when presented with an answer they were not expecting. The mark of a great leader is the ability to take a loss or rejection and turn it into something positive. Losing or being rejected is not failure in itself. Rather, true failure is a matter of how we choose to deal with that outcome. We see it all the time as leaders, whether it's our business that goes under, a major deal that falls apart, or a personal loss. How we manage and navigate in these intense and sometimes very emotional situations has a big impact on our future ability to lead others as well as stay in the game ourselves.

For any leader, rejection is a part of business. It's a part of *life*. Often we can't avoid it, but we *can* do something about it. The cycle starts when we are kids. I have seen my own sons, ages eleven and thirteen, try out for sports teams or school-related activities and sometimes fall short. The feeling of rejection can be devastating. They see their friends make the "A team" or be selected for a particular honor while one of them is left wondering why he couldn't make the cut. But each of them has also experienced winning, so they know the difference; and obviously "winning" is better. However, how we handle rejection or loss at such an early age is critical to shaping our response to it later in life. Obviously some people never figure out how to deal with it and wind up seeing themselves as victims with the odds stacked against them, which guarantees that they can never ultimately succeed, much less become a leader of others. Many have said that it's not what happens to you, but how you react to it that matters. This couldn't be truer than when, as a leader, you are dealing with a "no" in business or a professional situation, particularly when you've spent hours, days, and even weeks or months trying to land a particular client or account.

Clearly, no one wants to get a "no." However, despite the fact we all hear "no" more often than we'd like, it is the power of a positive—"I can and *will* deal with this"—attitude that will help us overcome any initial rejection so that we can switch our focus and energy to a more constructive and productive place. Consider the following leadership tips and tools for seeing the glass as half full instead of half empty:

- See rejection as an *opportunity* to grow and better understand what you could have done more effectively. We often get so close to our idea or proposal that we don't realize it's not connecting with our audience. Ask yourself if you're functioning and thinking on autopilot. Did you really consider the audience's point of view, or are you just so into it that you are "presenting for yourself," as I like to say. Is your presentation inundated with facts and figures that are boring or confusing to your audience? For any leader, taking the time to reassess your communication approach will likely produce better outcomes.

- As hard as it is, don't take the rejection personally. Very often, the receiver of your message is not rejecting you on a personal level but is saying "no" because of a variety of other reasons having to do with economics, market conditions, or internal factors in the organization. Though a positive attitude should have you feeling confident about yourself while always looking to improve your efforts, never lose sight of the fact that in business and in life, many decisions are beyond your control, so don't get so down on yourself. When a leader loses sight of this, he or she negatively impacts the entire team.

- Positive leaders proactively engage the person who rejected them. I say, be confident and secure enough to want to know why you were turned down so that you can fix it for the next time. Having a positive attitude puts you in the frame of mind to say, "Is there anything I need to know that can help me improve myself or my organization?" Again, there is a very strong correlation between having a positive, upbeat attitude and exuding confidence to all around you. Remember, great leaders are lifelong learners.

- Pick yourself up and dust yourself off. After you've had a chance to lick your wounds and find out as much as you can about why you got a "no," get right back on the horse.

Successful leaders, just like successful relief pitchers in baseball, have very short memories. If you obsess over a rejection or setback, you are likely to carry it with you when you are dealing with your next challenge. It may affect your judgment or decision making, which is deadly for a leader. Further, whining or complaining over a rejection will put you in a negative and counterproductive frame of mind. Remember that the next time you get a "no," which unfortunately for all of us is likely to be right around the corner.

- Resist the urge to blame others for a failing outcome. Why? Because it sounds like sour grapes. No one is inspired or motivated by hearing a leader say that it was someone else's fault why things didn't turn out right. Your team members as well as key stakeholders are looking to you for strength and moral support. They don't want to hear you complain as if you were a victim in all this. When they do, they only feel worse, which is the opposite of what strong leaders do.

- Gather yourself emotionally. Clearly, as a leader, having to keep it together and keep those around you together under such difficult circumstances as losing your business, an election, or a key client is never easy. Being rejected in any venue is highly emotional. However, even though it is okay to shed some tears, it is not okay to completely lose it. You can't fall apart to the point where your anger or despair takes control or you can't even speak because your emotions have gotten the best of you. I know it is easier said than done, but strong leaders must prepare for the distinct possibility that rejection or failure is very real and ask themselves beforehand, "How will I deal with losing, if it should occur?" Some would call this negative or pessimistic thinking. I disagree. I call it being *realistic*, being *prepared*. Obviously, you want to focus on the positive and what you need to do to succeed; however, to be totally unprepared for the possibility of coming up short is a leadership weakness. While you won't know exactly how you will react until it happens, it will be something you have thought through before that moment.

- Once your immediate disappointment and pain begin to subside, start to put your energy into figuring out how you can take this experience and learn from it. More specifically, write down exactly what you will and won't do, based on this loss or rejection, when faced with a comparable circumstance in the future. Doing this will have a powerful impact on your leadership style and ultimately increase your odds of being more successful next time around.

- Even when you fail, it is essential that team members know how much you appreciate their efforts. It is easy to do this when you win, but in many ways it is even more important that you share your appreciation when things don't turn out so well. Further, where appropriate, it is critical that you genuinely congratulate the winner or a fellow competitor who edged you out. Being gracious and dignified is essential in these circumstances because remember, you are not a failure as a person, but rather you have fallen short in this particular situation. As a leader, you will live to fight another day, so how you handle this situation is critical to how you will be perceived in the future when you inevitably get back in the game. Great leaders are resilient. Getting a "no" is only a temporary setback and an opportunity to grow and learn and come back stronger and smarter.

5

It's About *Them*

The Power of Empathy

As leaders, we often talk about how *we* see the world—*our* vision, *our* strategy, *our* plans. If we want to be truly great leaders, it's critical that we share how we see the world. We often criticize presidential candidates or those being considered as organizational CEOs for not having "the vision" to truly lead. However, well-rounded leaders must also have the ability—and a burning desire—to empathize and care about those they are trying to lead and serve. We need to genuinely care about our audience and our stakeholders, those who work for us and with us, those who report to us, those on our team, our peers. Simply put, those who help us achieve what we need to get done every day and allow us to get credit when things go right (and yes, if you are a really good leader, take responsibility when things go wrong).

The more we try to empathize with others, the more effective we can be in connecting with those same people in an effort to motivate and inspire them. That is exceptional leadership. We can talk about empathy, but the willingness to actually *demonstrate* empathy, requires a conscious decision to step outside yourself and imagine what it might be like to be in another person's shoes. Genuine empathy is less a leadership skill or some sort of technique or trait but more of an emotional and intellectual shift or adjustment that one comes to see as essential to fully evolve as a human being. I'm convinced you can't be a truly empathetic leader without being a truly empathetic person. It's hard to be one and not the other. Yet, being empathetic is no easy feat. It's really hard work, and it's not a 100 percent thing about which we are able to say, "Great, now I've got this empathy thing nailed down. . . . Next!"

On a personal note, I find that one minute I am focused on the needs and wants of others and very focused on what I call "other-centric" matters. When I do this I am remembering, "It's all about *them.*" Then, without understanding all the reasons for it (maybe because my PhD is not in psychology), another situation or circumstance will arise and it's as if I have blinders on. All I can see is what I want to see. All I see is what matters to me—my wants and needs. I become very "me-centric" and start living in the "it's all about *me*" world. When I get into this zone or this space, my ability to lead—and, in fact, deal effectively and harmoniously with those who matter in my world—is severely compromised. Let me share with you a couple of powerful yet embarrassing examples.

I wrote this chapter just a couple of days after Mother's Day. From my perspective, I did the appropriate things that a good husband should do for a great wife leading up to Mother's Day, like buying flowers, a nice gift, asking how I can help with the kids, etc. However, on the morning of Mother's Day, I hit the wrong note. My wife, Jennifer, is one of the most understanding and easygoing people you'll meet. Some of my friends will tell me that their wives or girlfriends complain that they "play too much golf" or "hang out with the guys too much." I've never heard my wife say anything like that, but on Mother's Day I proudly pronounced to my wife, "Jen, I've decided not to play golf today." "Great," she said. "What are you going to do?" I responded, "If it's okay with you, I'm going to the gym and then to Starbucks—just hang out and read the Sunday papers." That was the wrong answer, but Jen didn't say anything.

At the time, our then twelve-year-old son Nick was getting ready for a baseball game in the afternoon (imagine, a baseball game on

Mother's Day—talk about a lack of empathy on the part of the league!), at which I was serving as the assistant coach for his team. Our other son Chris, who was ten years old at the time, is a great kid but isn't much help around the house, and our daughter, Olivia, then four years old, is the cutest thing in the world but at times suffers from a chronic case of complaining and whining. *That* is what I left my wife with on Mother's Day morning while I went off to have a great workout and to read the Sunday papers at Starbucks.

I finally texted and said, "Jen, what time are we leaving for the game?" Politely she responded, "11:30." "Great," I said, but when I got back I could see something was wrong. Jen told me, "I had to rush to get Nick off to the game and the other two are driving me crazy. I never got the chance to get a workout myself." I said, "I'm sorry about that. I'll drive to the game . . ." but I could see I had at least one foot in the doghouse already. After the game, we went out to dinner and everything seemed fine. That was until our twelve-year-old son Nick said something that really hit me the wrong way. It wasn't that big a deal, but it irritated me and I let him know it. Once I told him how angry I was at him for doing and saying what he did (the details are irrelevant), I wouldn't let it go. I kept asking Nick why he did that particular thing, and when he didn't give me a straight answer I pressed him harder until he started crying. My wife sat patiently until finally she looked at me and said, "Really? Really, on Mother's Day you're gonna do this?"

I realized right at that moment how wrong I was. My giving Nick a hard time and my obsession about "being right" and his disobeying me were more important to me than thinking about the impact all this would have on our family and, most importantly, on Jennifer on Mother's Day. Of course I made things worse by politely but directly saying to her, "It would be nice if just once you took my side with the kids, because I always have your back." Well, that wasn't the right thing to say, nor was it especially empathetic. It was argumentative, petty, and selfish and just made things worse. I'll spare you the rest of the gory details but let's just say my inability to take a step back (both by overreacting to a ridiculously small situation with our son and by being inconsiderate when I failed to ask Jennifer what *she* wanted and needed to do on Mother's Day morning before I decided what was best for me) wound up creating a Mother's Day memory that frankly our entire family would rather forget. But I had to own it. I wished I could roll back the clock or the videotape and get a redo or, as we say in golf get a "mulligan" (a shot that doesn't count), but in life and in leadership it doesn't work that way.

How you react and respond in these instances has an impact on others not only in your personal life but also at work. You see, to make matters worse, while how I had mishandled Mother's Day was still on my mind, I compounded things the very next day by getting into another petty and totally unnecessary argument with my longtime business associate Mary Gamba. The argument was over something that had absolutely nothing to do with anything she had done wrong. We were simply going over something that had to be done at work, and I was feeling frustrated about *my* world, *my* screwup, *my* argument with my wife. All Mary was doing was what she always does, trying to get the job done in the most effective and efficient way possible with a smile on her face. Imagine the nerve of her! Again, the details surrounding the issue are irrelevant, but I wound up being contentious and argumentative with her for no good reason. It was all about me and my world—my frustration and guilt about something at home. I should have been focused on what Mary needed from me as a leader to accomplish what we needed to get done as a team and an organization. However, I didn't have what Daniel Goleman calls the "emotional intelligence" to step back, see the situation for what it was, and deal with things in a healthier, mature, and more empathetic fashion.[1]

Truly empathetic leadership requires that we constantly make a decision to step back and ask ourselves what is best for the other person in this moment in order to achieve the best possible results. When we don't do that and we instead allow our emotions to take control of us, we lead without a compass, which in turn leads us astray. What's worse, it creates human road kill, hurt feelings, and scars; and even after we apologize (which I did both to my wife and within minutes to Mary), it doesn't take away our initial actions.

Empathy is something we have to work at constantly; as I said, it's not something you check off on a box and say, "I've got this down!" Consider the following two cases that demonstrate just how much our leadership is impacted by our ability to empathize.

The Case of Con Ed: An "Inconvenience"—Really?

Our lack of empathy as individual leaders often manifests itself within large organizations that can have an impact on millions. When this happens, the lack of sensitivity and caring can have devastating effects not only on those on the wrong end of organizational actions but also on the reputation of the organization involved, not to mention the leaders who are so tone-deaf to the needs of the organization and who demonstrate an apparent lack of empathy for the people affected by decisions made or not made. Consider the widespread power outages in New York City in 2003 and the problems Con Edison had in getting that situation right. Thousands of residents were either without electricity or had "low voltage." Businesses lost money, and people suffered.

As they suffered, the usually able and competent then-mayor of New York, Michael Bloomberg, seemed to miss the mark on the situation. In fact, Bloomberg praised Con Ed's CEO Kevin Burke several days into the blackout and called the situation an "inconvenience" to those affected. Following these comments, the mayor took quite a bit of heat for what he said, and CEO Burke testified before government agencies that he wasn't sure what caused the blackouts nor was he sure what to do about it. So what does this mean for us? What can we learn from Con Ed's mistakes? Consider the following lessons:

- Some people are born with empathy, but for most of us it is something we must work at. It doesn't mean we are not concerned about other people, it means we really haven't thought through how to communicate that concern. I'm not convinced Michael Bloomberg and Kevin Burke didn't care about residents and businesses being without electricity. They didn't think it through clearly, step back, and imagine what it might be like to lose your power.

- I believe that either you care or you don't. I'm not convinced that people can be taught to care if they are truly insensitive. (There is no firsthand evidence that Bloomberg and Burke didn't care.) You could be exposed to things that open up your mind, but if at the core you are not emotionally connected, coaching won't help. Some leaders think their primary job is to be a manager who gets things done in an efficient way. But management and leadership are not the same thing. Real leadership is a lot more than simply doing things right. Sometimes it means doing the right thing in an ethical, compassionate, and empathetic fashion. That's a lot more complicated.

- There is a great book called *Bad Leadership: What It Is, How It Happens, and Why It Matters*, by Barbara Kellerman. In her book, Kellerman cites former New York City mayor Rudy Giuliani as an example of this. Kellerman says that before 9/11, Giuliani had a reputation for being a "my way or the highway" type of leader who was sometimes insensitive. In fact, when Amadou Diallo, an unarmed twenty-two-year-old West African immigrant, was shot at forty-one times by New York police, some argue that Giuliani showed little compassion. Said Kellerman in her book, "There was no heartfelt expression of sympathy from the mayor, nor much apparent empathy for the large number of his constituents who chafed under his leadership."[2]

  In April 2000, polls showed that only 32 percent of New York residents approved of Giuliani's handling of his job. But in the aftermath of 9/11, Giuliani showed an extraordinary degree of compassion and empathy. Apparently it was always there, but for whatever reason he couldn't or wouldn't show it until this tragic event. Now, many years later, Giuliani is considered to be one of the country's most respected leaders, not only because he was efficient but because he brought people together in the worst of times.

So what is the message for the rest of us? Show that you care, and don't hold back. You can be a tough leader, but do it with a warm heart. That doesn't make you weak; in fact, it makes you strong. Your people will see it, and your organization will greatly benefit.

Empathy Done Right: The Cleveland Clinic Video Series

Consider the words of Henry David Thoreau: "Could a greater miracle take place than for us to look through each other's eyes for an instant?" These are the words that begin a powerful and profound must-see video on YouTube simply titled, "Empathy: The Human Connection to Patient Care," which is part of a series of videos produced by the folks at the Cleveland Clinic a few years ago.[3] I heard about this video from a hospital administrator, who was referred to it by a nurse who said she sometimes "forgets why she does what she does" and in those cases tends to engage in a less than empathetic fashion with her patients and their families.

In the video, scenes of patients, hospital staff, visitors, and family members are shown with simple captions. Scenes include a woman on dialysis with the caption "Day 29 . . . Waiting for a new heart . . ." and a mother with her head down, "19-year-old son on life support." Another scene shows two men on an escalator, with the caption for the first man "Tumor was benign" and for the second man "Tumor was malignant." Then the video shows a wife and a young daughter along with the words "Husband is terminally ill . . . visiting dad for the last time." This extraordinary video ends on a powerful note with the caption, "If you could stand in someone else's shoes . . . Hear what they hear. See what they see. Feel what they feel. Would you treat them differently?"

That *is* the question. I encourage you to go to YouTube and watch the video. Virtually everyone who sees it has a visceral reaction. When I first saw it, I had a hard time keeping it together emotionally. But the part that is most profound from a leadership perspective is that the ability to empathize—in fact, the awareness of the need to empathize—is something we *must* remind ourselves of constantly. For the vast majority of us, we might see these same people in the exact same hospital setting and not think anything of what could be going on in their world and the impact it has on how they act and interact with others.

How many of us are turned off when we say hello to someone who doesn't respond. We are convinced they are rude when in fact they may have a "19-year-old son on life support." In reality, as leaders—and simply as human beings—we can't know for sure what is going on in the minds of those around us, but one of the biggest dangers in leadership is to become so consumed with our own reality that we become oblivious to the reality of those around us. We lose the ability and the willingness to even *try* to empathize with others. As a result, our relationships suffer, and in turn, our effectiveness suffers. When we later find out what was *really* going on with the other person, we often regret our initial reaction and say to ourselves, "If I had only known that was happening, I wouldn't have acted that way."

So consider a different approach in your efforts to build meaningful relationships with others, including colleagues, clients, and even adversaries. Give the other person the benefit of the doubt. If you are in a hospital, a meeting, a hallway, or even an elevator and a person looks despondent and not particularly friendly, ask yourself what *could* be going on that might cause such a reaction? As a leader, become more "other-centered." Ask an open-ended question in an effort to understand the other person's current mood or vantage point. It can be as simple as asking a colleague, "How are things going? I noticed you have been struggling with your deadlines. What can I do to help you?" Give him or her the option of opening up. Get into a conversation. Try to identify his or her needs. In the case of a client or prospect, consider asking, "How have your needs changed?" "What are your biggest challenges?" or "What's keeping you up at night?"

By showing concern or interest in others, you will interact and lead in a more compassionate and empathetic fashion. This takes a shift in thinking that requires you to be less focused on *your* circumstance in that moment and more focused on those around you.

In reality, you may not be able to understand *exactly* what the other person is feeling, but showing you care and demonstrating that you have taken the time to at least imagine what it would be like goes a long way. For some, this powerful lesson in leadership is a giant step indeed.

6

Oh No, Not Another Meeting!

Meetings matter—*a lot*. In any organization, the quality of meetings has a direct impact on productivity, effectiveness, and efficiency. Meetings also have a direct impact on employee engagement and happiness. Think about it. If your organization requires that you attend countless meetings that you find boring—and not especially relevant to you and your work—how engaged would you be? How satisfied with your job would you really be? What's so shocking to me, given my many years of leadership consulting and coaching, is how many deadly boring and poorly run meetings wind up becoming part of an organization's normal way of conducting business. Bad meetings simply become part of the organization's culture. "It's just the way we do things" is what I often hear as the explanation for these really bad meetings. But I don't buy it. Poor meetings are largely the product of poor leadership.

Bad meetings seep into the culture of any organization because its leaders don't know or care enough to change their meeting culture. Very often they lack the skills and tools—even if they do care—to do anything about it. Many leaders don't want to run uninspiring and rambling meetings that go on forever, but they do it anyway. Strong leaders must insist, however, that meetings are productive and dynamic as well as goal-oriented and concise. If you, like so many other leaders, feel inundated and distracted by the meeting mania going on in your organization, consider what I call a series of "organizational quality control" questions that can help you facilitate better, more productive meetings:

- What is the *goal* of this particular meeting? If you can't precisely and clearly state the meeting's goal in one sentence, something is seriously wrong. A meeting without a specific goal is a prescription for organizational problems. It's about the way you frame the purpose of the meeting. Try something like, "The goal of this meeting is to come up with three recommendations for improving the operations in our XYZ department."

- Exactly who needs to be in this very goal-oriented meeting and who doesn't? I know people who call everyone in their organization to virtually every meeting. This approach is rude and inconsiderate of people's time and energy. It turns people off and de-motivates them. Think about it. Who needs to be at a particular meeting, and what do they have to contribute? In answering this question, you are likely to find that you need only three to five people sitting around that table instead of ten to fifteen. More people at a meeting is rarely merrier.

- How prepared is the meeting leader to truly facilitate this session by asking clear, probing, and open-ended questions that move toward achieving your stated goal? If not, what training or coaching are you providing to help your meeting leaders be competent enough to run this important business activity?

- If the meeting is a so-called information-sharing session, is there a more efficient and cost-effective way of sharing such information? Simply put, if everyone in the meeting is going to be providing a report or update on their respective activities with no real discussion or follow-up, then why exactly does everyone need to be in a room listening to this? If all you are doing is dumping data, then instead ask each meeting participant to send a concise, one-page, bulleted e-mail with the key points they want to share with the group. As part of this e-mail, make sure that everyone on the team is given the opportunity to follow up with the messenger on any questions or issues they may have. Given today's technology, everyone doesn't have to be in the same room to share information. *Don't meet just to meet.*

• Finally, to what extent are you making sure that specific "action items" are being delivered and received as intended? If there is no action that comes out of the meeting, what was the point? Meetings must be about moving forward, and moving forward is about taking action and making decisions.

If more professionals and leaders engage in organizational quality control when it comes to meetings, the quality of our business lives (not to mention the quantity of time for our personal lives) would be greatly improved. Asking these questions is a critical step. Yet, the desire to lead better meetings only matters if you know how to do it. Given this, consider the following best practices to leading your next meeting that will make a *huge* difference in your organizations' overall effectiveness—not to mention employee engagement and satisfaction.

1 Have a goal-oriented agenda for every meeting. Put that agenda in writing and hand it out. There is nothing worse than getting together for a meeting and not being sure what the heck you're supposed to be trying to accomplish. Preparation for a meeting is critical.

2 Make sure the meeting's agenda is realistic. Don't put a million items on the agenda. You won't get through them. People will begin to count the agenda items and try and figure out how long the meeting will take. A long agenda wears people out. Fewer items dealt with in a realistic fashion are preferable to a laundry list of items you rush through. If word gets out that you run brief meetings in which things are actually

accomplished, most people won't grumble when you call a meeting.

3 Set the meeting's tone from the beginning. Start each meeting with an upbeat, positive, and welcoming attitude. Make it your business to greet each meeting participant by name ("Hi, Jim. How's it going?") as they walk into the room. Shake hands. Make small talk. Be warm and personable. Smile. Let people know you appreciate their being there. This approach is particularly important for meetings with an especially serious agenda.

4 Arrange the meeting room so that everyone can see the other participants. I like to use a round table or a semicircular arrangement. This promotes eye contact and more personal interaction.

5 Tell participants how long the meeting will last. Start on time and end on time. People will really appreciate that.

6 Stay on track. So many meetings get sidetracked because the leader allows participants to go off on tangents. Worse, the leader goes off on tangents. (I have been guilty of this on occasion.) Remind participants what you are there to accomplish. Set boundaries for discussion, but not with an iron fist. Say, "That's a great point, Bob. But time is limited and we need to get back on track. Maybe we can discuss your point in private or at another meeting."

7 Be an active listener. Pay attention to each person's comments and acknowledge their participation: "Mary, your point is well taken. I think it helps us see the situation in a different light. Thanks."

8 Summarize the decisions reached during the meeting at the end. As I mentioned earlier, meetings must be about moving forward, taking action, and making decisions. Thus, it is critical that you make it clear what action is to be taken afterward. This cuts down on people going off with different interpretations of what happened during the meeting. It also validates the meeting and reminds people that you don't call meetings just to meet.

So what is the leadership lesson in all of this? Simply put, meetings can be productive, engaging, and extremely useful, *or* they can be boring and de-motivating and waste valuable time. Great leaders choose to lead great meetings. It does not happen by accident. They make a conscious decision to make the most of the time they have with their team, and the payoff is huge.

7

Listen, Really Listen!

In the course of my asking well over two hundred leaders of all stripes to identify the number-one leadership lesson they have learned in their respective careers, a significant number of them told me that it is the ability to truly listen that matters most. Many of their responses discussed how much they learned by being a good listener, how they made better decisions involving organizational problems they were able to view in a different light, and how they wound up identifying opportunities—all because they listened to the point of view of others. Leaders who truly listen also know that much of their organization's success is built on strong relationships—both inside the organization and with key external stakeholders and industry experts. Yet, none of this happens if those relationships don't involve great listening. For example, when leaders really listen to their people internally, it makes those same employees feel valued and has the potential to reduce stress during difficult situations and boost morale.

There is little doubt that there are many reasons why being a great listener is a powerful leadership lesson. Yet, there are many misconceptions about what it really means for a leader to be a good listener. Listening is not simply hearing what someone is saying. For any leader, being a really good listener requires that you be anything but passive or silent throughout an entire conversation. In fact, if you are silent or passive for too long, it can easily send the message to the other party that you are uninterested and disengaged. Simply being silent while another person is speaking without interjecting encouraging comments ("That's really interesting") or asking follow-up questions ("Why do you think that?") is what I've come to call "lazy listening." Conversely, the kind of listening that a truly exceptional leader engages in is active, responsive, and in the moment. It requires a genuine desire to develop a better understanding not only of what is being said but also the person who is saying it. Further, the kind of listening I'm talking about can also involve a leader trying to understand *why* what is being said is being said in the first place. It requires a much deeper level of commitment than simply being silent when someone is talking but rather a level of concentration and engagement in the conversation that takes hard work.

Being this type of leader who listens in such an active and present fashion is more challenging than ever for some. Distractions are everywhere: smartphones, tablets, instant messages. We are "pinged" so constantly that it is more difficult than ever to truly be in the moment and able to listen at the levels needed to rise above these distractions. I've come to the conclusion that listening at the level necessary to be really great at this is never going to happen until—and unless—a leader makes a fully conscious decision that the effort to cut out these distractions is really worth it. Further, this same leader must also understand that not making this commitment to truly listen has the potential to produce serious consequences, not only for the leader but for the organization.

In fact, one company I've worked with actually requires its managers to attend meetings with their laptops or handheld device so that they can remain constantly connected. What message are organizational leaders sending when they do this? Basically, they are saying that for those who attend the meeting, listening to what is being said is not any more important than whatever else is going on around them. These leaders are also clearly saying that the so-called other work that meeting attendees are involved in is in fact more important than the meeting agenda itself. So attendees might ask, why are we even having a meeting in the first place if we don't really have to listen to what is going on?

Further, I have several clients who hold meetings in which each attendee is expected to bring a laptop. The objective is for each PowerPoint presentation delivered by meeting participants to be followed by others in the meeting via this technology. Consider the problem with this approach: to what degree can each attendee actually be listening and engaged with the presenter standing in front of the room if their eyes and their attention are focused on the technology at their seat? Simply put, there is no eye contact with the presenter. Therefore, the level of listening taking place is seriously compromised, because while meeting participants might hear what is being said, they could miss facial expressions, hand gestures, or other contextual cues that truly embody the experience of the presentation being shared.

Ultimately, the question has to be asked, why is the presentation being made at all if the others in the meeting are simply following the PowerPoint presentation on their laptops and not truly listening to and observing the presenter in the first place? The point here is that truly engaged and active listening is hard enough without organizational leaders making conscious and so-called strategic decisions that make it even more difficult.

Consider the following: it is said that 85 percent of what we know we learn through listening. Further, 70 to 80 percent of our typical business day as leaders is spent engaging in some form of communication. When you break this down, 45 percent of this time is spent listening, 30 percent speaking, 16 percent reading, and 9 percent writing.[1]

These are just some of the compelling reasons to make the effort to be a better listener and, ultimately, a better leader. Yet, in spite of this overwhelming evidence, there are so many professionals in positions of leadership that just don't get it and in turn actively send the message that they are simply too distracted and uninterested to listen.

Sometimes, Actions Speak Louder Than Words

Consider Betty, a marketing and public relations professional, who works in a major family-owned business. I've been in numerous business meetings with Betty and her uncle, John, in which Betty is supposed to be actively participating and listening to important content. Questions are asked, decisions are made, and input is needed, requiring everyone in the meeting to be truly engaged and listening at the highest level. Yet, Betty has taken out her iPhone and has started e-mailing or texting (does it really matter which one?) in virtually every one of these meetings. Every time Betty does this, she sends the message that she is not listening because someone or something on the other end of that iPhone is more important than the people in the business meeting or the subject matter of the meeting itself.

The first time I witnessed this behavior in a meeting with Betty and her uncle, I was with Mary Gamba, vice president of marketing and client relations at our leadership consulting firm Stand & Deliver. Now, Mary is an exceptional listener—one of the many reasons she has grown as a leader in our organization over the years. Before I could even comment on Betty's conduct, Mary said to me with an incredulous look, "Can you believe how Betty handled herself in that meeting? She wasn't listening at all. She was too busy texting, e-mailing, and playing with her phone. How is she supposed to follow up on the items we discussed in the meeting, and how are we supposed to move forward? She is our point person and clearly missed most of what we were talking about because she simply wasn't listening!"

As Mary and I talked more about Betty and her poor listening skills, we agreed that what we saw in her was not isolated, but rather a serious problem for many professionals in leadership positions. You could say that the issue of poor listening is bordering on a leadership epidemic with serious consequences.

Ten Keys to Active and Engaged Listening

With this backdrop, consider my top ten keys, for you as a leader, to becoming a more active and engaged listener:

1 Get yourself in the right frame of mind to listen. I call it my "listening mode." The key here is to go into meetings and conversations with a more open mind. Think of the times that you've actually learned something new or have considered an issue or situation from a perspective other than your own simply because you were listening. Often, we forget our past experiences and go into autopilot as leaders. When we do this, we forget the importance of keeping an open mind. Yet, when we work to find a reason to listen, there is usually a big payoff. Further, if you've worked really hard as a leader to surround yourself with the best and the brightest professionals, why wouldn't you be open to really listening to them? If you did anything other than this, you would be shortchanging yourself as a leader as well as your organization by losing out on the benefit of that wisdom and expertise.

2 Concentrate. Let's not kid ourselves. This is hard stuff. Again, I'm not talking about simply hearing what is said, but listening. Don't concentrate on what you are preparing to say in response or in rebuttal to what you think is being said. When you do this, you tend to miss important information. This is what I call "listening defensively." In some ways, listening defensively and getting ready to fight back feels more natural for many of us, not only as leaders but as human beings. I admit it is often my first instinct, but it's the wrong instinct in the vast majority of cases. Why? Because this behavior often comes from a place of vulnerability and insecurity and not from a position of strength. We listen defensively and prepare our response because we're convinced—very often in heated or challenging conversations—that we want to be right; or worse, that we *need* to be right. When we do this, it's almost impossible to listen at the level required to really

understand what another person is saying and, more importantly, why they're saying it.

3 Fight the urge to interrupt. It's really irritating to the other person. Think of how you feel when it is done to you. This is the best reason to avoid being a constant interrupter, because it feels terrible when you're on the other end of it. I'm not talking about the kind of interrupting that is encouraging and supportive, which I'll cover in more detail in my next tip, but rather the kind of interrupting that sends the message that you're just not interested in what the other person is saying. When you interrupt in this way, you fail to encourage the other person to open up and share more, and you are in fact discouraging them. For a leader, shutting other people down is dangerous indeed.

4 Use encouraging comments in conversation. These include "Tell me more . . ." or "What happened next?" or "Why do you see it that way?" Don't be a pest, but send the message that you are truly interested in what is being said and want to know more. Acknowledge the other person. He or she will tend to open up and share with you. You can't use encouraging comments effectively, at the right time and in the right place in a conversation, unless you are truly engaged and listening at the highest level. When you do, you will be amazed at how much you can find out and learn; and for a leader, this is an extraordinary gift.

5 Be an "active listener" in conversations or meetings. As I've said before, being a good listener doesn't mean you have to shut your mouth entirely. Occasionally paraphrase what you think someone is saying: "So, what you're saying is . . ." or "I just want to be clear on this." Be empathetic. By doing this you are acknowledging the other person and what he or she is saying. Paraphrasing is a powerful leadership tool. It not only gives the other person a chance to respond to what you said but also sends the message that you, as a leader, care enough to listen to that person so intently and that you're putting in the effort to determine what's really being said. As a leader,

helping the other person sense that you actually care can ultimately have an extremely positive impact on your relationship.

6 Practice patience. Take a deep breath or two. As I said earlier, don't interrupt. Further, try not to finish the other person's sentences. I can't tell you how many times I've done this and found out I was wrong about what the other person was going to say. Plus, even if you're right, it's a turnoff. The key here is to simply *shut up*! This is where great listening does require silence. You get points for accurately finishing someone else's sentence, and the other person is likely to resent you for it. It is their story, not yours. It is their part of the conversation, not yours. It is their solution to the problem, not yours. Smart leaders know that being smart doesn't mean you need to be the "smartest kid in the class." Rather, the key is to make other people feel like *they* are "the smartest kid in the class." The irony is that smart leaders who understand this lesson also know that much of their success comes from how other people feel when they are interacting with them, and a lot about how people feel is based on whether they think you are listening to them or not. So remember that the next time you are about to finish someone else's sentence because you're convinced you know what they're going to say and want to be the one to say it first.

7 Keep your eyes on the other person. Fight the urge to look around the room. Sure, there are distractions, but when you make a decision to listen with your mind and body, you will be amazed at your ability to concentrate. I'm not advocating that you stare, like some sort of nut. Rather, simply let the other person know that you are present with them. Focused, steady eye contact is big. Further, a leader who is listening over the phone can often be tempted to multitask because he or she can't be seen. I've done it and I've paid the price—not only by missing a key word or phrase, but also by missing the nuance of what is being said. It's like playing Russian roulette; and for a leader with a lot on the line, it's not worth it. Shut off the computer. Take your smartphone and turn it

face down. Take the papers on your desk and set them aside. Imagine that the people on the call can, in fact, see everything you are doing. Ultimately, as I've said earlier in this chapter, make the decision as a leader that the benefits of being truly engaged and focused as a listener far outweigh whatever you think you can gain by multitasking during a call.

8 Find common ground with the other person. Find out a few things about the other person before you start talking. Bring up things that both of you share—family, sports, education, background, previous jobs, and so on. This isn't a gimmick. It is a must-have tool in your leadership toolkit and is a very real way of getting to know someone before you start "talking business." It breaks the ice and makes it easier to relate to each other.

9 Use your body language to show your interest. Lean toward the speaker instead of slouching back. Keep your arms and hands open and relaxed. Never cross your arms if you want to send the message that you are listening and want to know more. As a fellow columnist, Carol Kleiman, once wrote, "Body language often speaks loudest."[2] Once again, consider the body language of Betty in the meeting I discussed earlier. It spoke volumes, even when she wasn't talking. Yet, the sad part is I'm betting she had no idea—and still doesn't—as to the impact of her nonverbal messages, not just in that meeting but in countless others.

10 Finally, try not to judge the speaker. We get so caught up on whether or not we agree with the other person's point of view, we tend to miss opportunities to truly understand what he or she is saying. It is not that important that we agree. What is important is that we connect on a human and personal level. That's about understanding. That's about trust. Ultimately, that's about leadership.

8

Great Leaders Ask Great Questions

Often great leadership comes down to asking great questions. In her book *Change Your Questions, Change Your Life*, my colleague Dr. Marilee Adams identifies what she calls "worried questions," such as "Does he like and approve of me?" or "What did I do wrong?" Dr. Adams also refers to "judging questions" that leaders use, which often, unnecessarily, put those around them on the defensive.[1] When things go wrong in our organizations, some of us ask questions like "Who screwed this up?" or "What could you possibly have been thinking when you did that?" To be clear, I'm a big advocate of confronting situations head-on—dealing with things before they get worse. How leaders go about confronting is key to what happens next and, ultimately, how difficult situations are resolved—or not.

These questions—the worried and judging ones—put people in a position to either fight back or clam up. I know I've been in both positions, as I write about in detail in chapter 3 of this book. Growing up the son of a very successful and dedicated but incredibly tough and aggressive father, who was the leader of a large and complex nonprofit organization (I explain in detail in the preface why

74

I feel he is such a complex and fascinating leader), I was often on the defensive—fighting to protect myself in any way I could—from my father's accusatory questions and his potential wrath. I came to understand years later that my father led and parented in the only way he knew how. It's the way his father was with him. My father rarely wanted to have a conversation about a particular situation or hear my version of things. (Often I was trying to explain one screwup or another on my part or simply wanting to tell him that I wanted to be more independent from him and the organization he built.) My father's questions—the questions of many leaders who can be impatient and aggressive—can be de-motivating to those around us.

In her book, Dr. Adams argues that these questions often come from an insecure, vulnerable place in us. They actually signal weakness. They are negative in nature and often cause you to lead in defensive and unnecessarily combative terms. When you formulate these questions in your mind and then actually articulate them, the ensuing conversation rarely goes anyplace good. Let's talk "worried questions" in greater detail as Dr. Adams describes them.[2]

Too many of us in the world of business, particularly in these difficult economic times, obsess over worried questions, such as "Why didn't he call me back about that proposal?" . . . "I haven't been able to get on Jim's schedule. Does that mean he doesn't want to do business with me?" . . . "What if I screw up this big presentation?" These questions are natural. They are in all of us. However, the key to successful leadership, which boosts productivity and your bottom line, is to *realize* that you are thinking this way. Then, immediately change your frame of mind because if you don't, you will have zero chance of a positive outcome. In her book, Dr. Adams promotes what she calls "helping questions." These questions center on how you can solve problems and move forward. Consider questions like "How can we get to the next step?" . . . "What can we do to overcome this obstacle?" . . . "What exactly do you need from me?"

As leaders, no matter what situation we face in our professional lives, whether rejection, disappointment, or anything that doesn't go exactly the way we had planned, the key is to train ourselves to move toward these helping questions, because the sooner we ask them, the more likely we are to stay on track. Too many of us focus our leadership on finding the right answers and anticipating the questions or objections that may be raised by others. Being prepared in this way is appropriate, but it can't be the only approach to solving problems and challenges.

Now, let's take a closer look at the issue of asking what Dr. Adams calls "judging questions."[3] She argues compellingly that as leaders we have a choice—countless times every day—as to the type of questions we will ask when things go wrong. Earlier in my career as a leader, I often functioned from a mindset that said I had to find out "who screwed up," and I often went to great lengths to find this out. I would sometimes act more like a prosecutor interrogating my team members—as well as family members—with probing and accusatory questions. It was a style I had learned as a child and had seen my father perfect over many decades—and he accomplished great things that have had a great impact on many people, as I describe in detail in the preface of this book.

But, like so many leaders, I didn't realize the negative impact this approach could have on my team members—or worse, I really didn't want to take such a hard look at myself as a leader, given that I was supposed to be a leadership and communication "expert." In fact, in many ways, Dr. Adams's book *Change Your Questions, Change Your Life*, marked a major turning point in my evolution as a leader.

Instead of being a "judger" as a leader, Adams offered a better and much more effective approach to asking questions. Why not be a leader who sees every situation or circumstance as an opportunity to learn? Why not take the "I want to learn more" approach, especially when things don't go as planned. Instead of assuming someone screwed up and that you as a leader are charged with the responsibility of prosecuting the case against that person—why not have a more open, positive, and solution-oriented mindset? When leaders use questions as tools to find out important information, they make better decisions. They also create an environment where those around them feel that they are more interested in finding a solution than pointing the finger of blame. Leaders who ask learning questions build stronger and healthier relationships with team members, who in turn are more likely to provide candid and helpful information and feedback about difficult and challenging situations.

As leaders, we know logically—instinctively—which approach to asking questions is likely to produce the best possible outcome. Yet, as is the case with so many leadership best practices or lessons, knowing what to do and actually doing it are two very different things. Full disclosure: just as I was working on this chapter on how great leaders ask learning questions, I was guilty of falling into the trap of asking accusatory and unnecessarily judging questions that have made a difficult situation worse. I've done it as a leader in my professional life with colleagues and I've also done it in my personal life with family—most notably with my wife, Jennifer, about one of the many domestic issues that couples deal with in the course of life, including not just going through a major renovation of our primary home but also building a second home down at the Jersey Shore. I share this to say that all of us, even those who want to see ourselves as strong leaders or well-rounded people, lose focus as to how we should be conducting ourselves and the questions we should be asking. Asking the right questions in difficult situations is a constant choice. A constant challenge to be aware of what is happening as it's happening and, perhaps most important, pausing— even stopping—taking a deep breath before you say or do anything and asking yourself a couple of critical questions, such as "What exactly is my goal in this situation?" and "What are the best questions I can ask that will help move in that direction?"

I know it's not easy in the heat of the moment. I've been there. We all have. We will all be there again. But the constant challenge we all have—not just as leaders but as imperfect human beings who try to learn from the past and evolve into our best selves—is to see the fork in the road, the choices before us, and decide to take the path that offers the chance to reach a better solution. I'm talking about becoming a more focused leader who wants to *learn* not only *what* happened but *why* it happened and wants to understand what the best options are in order to move forward in a positive way.

Great leaders ask great questions focused on learning more, and doing this on a consistent basis is the goal that all of us should aspire to every day. But what are the keys and the techniques to asking really good questions that get the other person to open up? Here are some lessons that should prove helpful:

- Make sure your questions are clear and easy to understand. Sounds simple, right? Then why is it that too often, people will ask a question and you have no idea what they want to find out? Before you ask a question, make sure you know why you are asking it. (P.S. Don't ask a question just to be heard. It's irritating.)
- Direct your questions to a particular person. You are more likely to get a direct response. Questions asked of a particular person are more effective than simply asking a generic question of an entire group. Often, when questions are asked of an entire group, people are reluctant to be the first to speak up. Also, it makes it easier for audience members to hide and not participate.
- Ask one question at a time. Don't you hate those multi-part questions? How do you know which part you are supposed to answer first? Do you ever find that you can't remember what the first part was? Ask one question, on one subject, to one person and you'll be pleased with the results.
- Follow up on a previous question that has been answered. Something like, "Jane, how does your answer compare with what Jim said on this subject earlier in the meeting?" Another effective follow-up is a short encouraging comment after someone has responded to an initial question, like "How so?" or "For example . . . ?"
- Don't be unnecessarily combative, unless you have a good reason for doing so. Avoid questions like "Why is it that you never seem to get it right, Bob?" If you are looking to scare

the heck out of Bob or let him know he is about to be fired, you've succeeded. Questions like this can cause real problems.

So the next time you are in a situation where someone says something that rubs you the wrong way, or something gets screwed up—which it inevitably will—fight the urge to ask a combative, negative, and judging question like "What's wrong with you?" or "How could you say that?" or even worse, "Are you some kind of idiot?" Go in a different, more constructive direction in an effort to learn more and ask "Tell me, why do you see it that way?" or "What can I do to move things forward?" or simply "How can I be helpful?" You will be amazed at the reaction you get using this simple but powerful leadership, and frankly human, approach that revolves, not around answers, but once again around asking the right questions, in the right way, for the right reasons.

9

Great Leaders Build Future Leaders

We all need mentors at critical points in our professional lives. None of us would have succeeded to the degree we have without the advice, guidance, and encouragement of key mentors. Simply put, we don't do it alone. I have been fortunate enough to have had numerous mentors who have been so helpful to me as a leader in training. Further, being a mentor is a critical component of a leader's role. Our success as leaders is often judged on how effective we are in mentoring and developing others. It's not good enough that you become the best at what *you* do. That's not a complete leader; that's an expert, and there is a huge difference between the two. Great leaders leave a legacy, and that legacy is in large part based on the degree that those whom we have coached, developed, and mentored have made their own mark.

Yet, many leaders say they face a multitude of challenges mentoring others: "Not enough time" . . . "The person I'd like to mentor doesn't directly report to me" . . . "You invest so much in people who sometimes end up leaving you in the end"—so many excuses for why mentoring is so challenging. Yet, the price we pay—the price our organization pays—can be devastating and demoralizing when we don't meaningfully invest the time and effort it takes to mentor others. Plus, when we don't mentor or coach selected people on our team, we as leaders lose out on the immensely gratifying and rewarding experience of seeing "our people" grow, fall, get back up, and ultimately reach their professional (and at times personal) potential.

With all this in mind, consider the following leadership lessons, along with very practical mentoring and coaching tips and techniques, which will make a big difference in your efforts to develop those around you:

- Catch people on your team doing things right. Often as leaders and managers, it is so easy to jump on people when they make a mistake. I know I do it more often than I should. Of course, we need to respond and deal directly with performance issues, but at the same time, we must be vigilant in recognizing and celebrating when team members succeed. Mentoring is about communicating to people what they did *right*, why it is important to the team, and what specific behavior needs to be replicated in the future and why. For example, "David, I want you to know that I really like the way you handled the Jones project. You were calm and reasonable when some others might have overreacted. Good job." If a leader fails to communicate in this fashion, the team member will fail to be motivated or inspired, which is a missed opportunity not just for the leader but for the entire team.
- Put people in a position to succeed. Think through the respective strengths and weaknesses of those on your team. Avoid putting people in positions just because you need to "fill a slot." Smart leaders identify the best writers and then put those people in positions to write on behalf of the team. Poor leaders take very weak writers and insist that they write and then are continually frustrated when a poor work product is delivered. Of course, we need to develop people in areas where they can improve; however, this should not be done by putting them in a position to fail. Consider people with poor interpersonal skills who don't like interacting with others being put in

charge of customer service. That would be ridiculous. Instead, take the person who is highly personable and put *that* person in charge of customer service. It sounds simple, but many leaders fail to get this mentoring step right.

- Push the envelope. It is essential that a mentor exude confidence in a mentee's potential. One of the best things someone can say about a leader who has helped develop him is "He believed more in me than I believed in myself." When a mentee sees that you have confidence in him and his ability, it has the potential to cause him to be more confident. Why? Because the mentee figures, "If someone so successful thinks I am capable of accomplishing this task, then maybe the mentor is right."

- Stay with it. Even if the mentee gets defensive when you deliver hard-to-hear feedback, it is essential that you make it clear that you are being direct about her performance "because I care about you and your future. The only way you are going to get better is by having hard conversations like this." Stick with it, even if you don't get the reaction you'd like at first. Effective mentoring is definitely a marathon, not a sprint. Funny, the same thing is true when it comes to being a great leader.

- Identify specific areas for improvement. Clearly identify specific goals and actions your mentee needs to work on. Further, clarify *why* the need for a change exists. It is critical that he sees that there is a problem or a potential crisis, as opposed to your telling him he needs coaching. People need to understand what you are trying to accomplish and why. This is particularly true of organizations undergoing significant change. In this situation, beyond employees, partners, and customers, all shareholders need to understand where the organization is going and how they are invested in the outcome.

- Remember that mentoring is a two-way street. It is one thing to send a message about specific goals that *you* would like a mentee to accomplish, but it is critical that the mentee is given the opportunity to tell you what she thinks is important. As a leader, ask your mentee about her professional goals. Ask about challenges, frustrations, and yes, feelings and emotions.

To be a great mentor, a leader must make a human and personal connection with the mentee. If a mentor is driving the entire process and setting the goals, without the active participation of the mentee, there won't be sufficient buy-in or engagement. That's why creating a dynamic conversation is critical to effective mentoring.

- Be a great listener. Part of creating a two-way street is about listening. Like leadership, coaching and mentoring must be a dialogue, not a monologue. Learn to ask engaging, open-ended questions. Go in to your first coaching session with a team member with a specific set of questions, such as: "What do you think is getting in the way of your ability to perform more effectively?" "How much passion and enthusiasm do you really feel about the work you are doing?" "What would make you more committed not to just the job but to our team?" If you don't get an answer right away, relax. Allow for the silence that so many teachers and others dread. Wait patiently for a response. Silence and the thinking that hopefully goes with it can be a powerful part of the mentoring process.
- Don't be a know-it-all. Being a great coach and mentor is as much about listening as it is about resisting the urge to be the expert who has all the answers. Self-disclosure has its place, but as a coach you can do too much of it. Watch how often you say things like "If I were in your situation, I would . . ." or "I remember a time I had the same problem." The key is to keep asking probing questions that help the employee come up with specific solutions on his own. The focus is not on you as the smartest person in the room or on the team, but rather on the people who need to better understand what needs to be done. Further, don't do "data dumps." As a leader, it is important that you don't simply pass out information. Your goal should be to get people to think for themselves and ask the right questions. They can't do that if leaders are spoon-feeding them the so-called right answers. Consider the adage, "Give a man a fish, and he'll eat for a day. Teach him how to fish, and he'll eat for a lifetime."

- Set and clarify expectations. Immediately after a coaching session with an employee, it is your job to generate a brief, bullet-point summary of what was just agreed to. This is critical for the employee to stay on track—and for you as a coach—to have a specific, action-oriented agenda for the next face-to-face coaching session. Without such summaries, the coach and the employee could have very different interpretations of what was just agreed to in a session.
- Have passion for what you teach as well as for those you are trying to teach and learn from. Passion can't be faked. Employees know whether you care or not. Great mentors and leaders teach from the heart.

Effective Mentors Give Constructive Feedback

One of the keys to being an effective leader and mentor is to give your people valuable constructive feedback. Yet, in my own leadership consulting and coaching work, I have found that a significant number of clients struggle to give the kind of feedback their direct reports really need. Consider these valuable tips that can help in this regard:

- When giving feedback, be as specific as possible. For example, "Mary, you did a great job on the Jones report. Let's take it a step further. I noticed that you didn't go into great detail on what you think our options are. Next time, make concrete recommendations that evaluate the costs and the risks." The key is to give people information that they can do something with. Conversely, if you say, "Way to go on the Jones report, Mary." That's okay to a point, but sooner or later Mary needs to know exactly what she needs to do to improve her performance and contribute to the team in a more productive fashion.
- Avoid judgmental comments. For example, "Mary, you need to be more enthusiastic about working here. Your casual attitude

is starting to affect your work." First of all, what exactly does "enthusiastic" mean? That's a very subjective word. Further, how exactly is Mary's lack of enthusiasm affecting her work performance? The problem is that the leader/coach has said nothing that Mary can use to improve her performance. Further, such "you need to" statements can cause many people to become unnecessarily defensive. Instead, ask the team member a probing question that gives them the opportunity to explain the behavior you have been observing without coming across as judgmental. An important lesson to remember is— ask before you assume.

- Give feedback face-to-face. Sure, e-mail, faxes, and phone messages can complement your coaching efforts, but the most powerful and effective feedback is usually in person. When face-to-face with team members, you can read their body language and attempt to interpret their reaction to your feedback. It's hard to do that when you are communicating via technology. In any case, the coaching I do via phone or video conference is effective only once a face-to-face personal connection has been well established.

- Keep a positive attitude. If someone on your team is falling behind or has missed a deadline, you might ask, "What obstacles or issues are keeping you from meeting the goals we agreed on?" The key here is to frame the feedback in a positive fashion, as opposed to assigning blame or fault.

- Give feedback as quickly as you can. Too often, leaders and managers wait too long to talk to an employee about something they are concerned about. The problem is that your feedback often gets lost. This is particularly true when trying to give positive feedback—recognize people's efforts immediately. However, according to Marty Brounstein, the author of *Coaching and Mentoring for Dummies*, "When giving negative feedback, you may want to apply a different timeline: ASAR (as soon as reasonable/ready—that is, when you're ready)." According to Brounstein, there are times when incidents happen that leaders need some time to cool off and get their thoughts together before dealing with the situation.[1] I agree with Brounstein to a point, but I have also found that when I'm delivering feedback on presentations to clients, my coaching advice, including the need for improvement, is more effective when given in real time.

What About Performance Reviews?

Clearly, one of the keys to being a successful leader when it comes to coaching and mentoring is engaging your people in a direct, candid, and constructive fashion regarding their performance. Historically, so-called performance reviews have not achieved this objective. Too often, these reviews provide little, if any, tangible feedback that allows employees to improve their performance in specific areas. This lack of candid dialogue about employee performance can only produce a culture of mediocrity at best. At worst, it produces cynicism and apathy toward the employee evaluation process.

A few years ago I was coaching Jim, a partner in a regional law firm, about this issue. Jim had conducted a seminar for new firm managers about the need to be more candid and direct in employee evaluations. The firm's concern was that too many managers were liberally doling out evaluations of 3s and 4s on a scale from 1 to 5, with 1 being poor performance and 5 being exceptional. According to Jim, many managers felt giving their people 3s and 4s was the "safest" thing to do because it wouldn't require any detailed explanation. Further, even though some employees deserved an evaluation of 2, managers were avoiding this at all costs. Who needs all that aggravation, right?

Finally, through Jim's coaching and mentoring, he convinced a second-year manager named Linda to give an evaluation of 2 to one of her people, named Jane. Linda also provided a detailed, written explanation attempting to justify this evaluation, which simply stated "needs improvement." Not only did Linda put the 2 in writing, but it only reinforced what she had been verbally sharing with Jane on many occasions over the past year. However, once the evaluation of "needs improvement" was actually put in writing, all hell broke loose. Jane challenged it saying she "had no idea where this was coming from." Further, she went to another partner in the firm to complain, stating, "If this stands, I refuse to work on any client under Linda's direction." So much for accepting constructive feedback in a positive way.

According to Jim, "It is absolutely essential that the organization take a firm stand. In great organizations, in order to achieve excellence and stay there and grow, you have to be candid, honest, and sometimes share hard-to-hear feedback about the performance of your people, especially when specific improvement is needed. Without that, you have no right to expect success."

Jim is absolutely right, and his law firm faced a critical test. If Jane was able to have her way and get her performance appraisal upgraded and, further, opt out of any assignments reporting to Linda, then the message would be sent loud and clear that the firm does not take employee performance seriously. However, if the firm's leadership decided to take a hard line and communicate, not just in words but in actions, that they expect and require their managers to provide specific, constructive, and candid feedback about where their people must improve, then the firm will be on the right track to success.

In the movie *A Few Good Men*, the lawyer played by Tom Cruise famously demands that the colonel played by Jack Nicholson tell the truth, to which the colonel angrily responds, "You can't handle the truth." While we all know that scene, the question for us as leaders is this: Are we willing to share the truth as we see it, when it comes to employee performance? Or are we going to go with inflated and bogus evaluations that have little value in helping team members improve and grow? That is a critical question that not only will determine our success as leaders but will have a tremendous impact on the development of our people and on the success of our team.

Regardless of what we do professionally, the only way we can truly improve our performance and leadership is to receive and accept critical feedback without being defensive or argumentative.

Exceptional leaders recognize this and are committed to providing constructive feedback to help their team members grow. When leaders do this well, they help develop the leaders of the future and weed out those who can't or won't lead. Both outcomes are keys to organizational success.

10

Receiving Feedback

Can You Handle the Truth?

As previously stated in this book, feedback, particularly if it is negative or critical, is always hard to hear. Leadership experts talk all the time about the importance of giving employees feedback on their performance. However, when it really comes down to it, how candid or honest are most performance reviews? How directly do most leaders communicate when certain employees aren't getting the job done? How specific do we get when we talk to individuals about exactly how they need to improve and why? Further, to what degree do we as leaders do this with the sense of urgency that the situation requires?

Recently, I taught a leadership seminar at a local university. Because I had to shorten the session a little to attend my young son's first baseball game, I neglected to ask the seminar participants to complete the usual written instructor evaluation. I, of course, assumed that I did a solid job and that my interactive presentation style and approach resonated with most, if not all, students.

However, I later found out that this was not the case. In fact, in a very hard-to-listen-to conversation, a prominent dean at the university told me that several students were "put off" by my ending the seminar early, as well as by what he described as my "in-your-face" style. I was shocked. My immediate reaction was to defend myself, but the dean insisted that something must have been different with my teaching style in this particular seminar series, since the student evaluations at the same university before this were really positive.

There is a huge leadership lesson here, one that I had to learn the hard way. It is easy to receive feedback such as "You are doing a great job, Joe, keep it up" or "Steve, we loved your seminar and your engaging and energetic teaching style." However, some of the most valuable and constructive feedback we can receive is critical of our performance. It tells us what others perceive in terms of where we fell short.

It doesn't matter if you are in a university classroom leading a group of students or a leader of your company's department. The only way to truly improve your performance (regardless of what you do professionally) is to receive and accept critical feedback without being defensive or argumentative and figure out how to improve or revise your leadership approach. As I said, feedback is a funny thing. It is easy to accept positive feedback, because it reinforces how we want to be perceived in the eyes of others. But the truly great presenter and leader is a person who can accept and in fact embrace the feedback that is hard to hear. It's not easy, I know.

Let me provide another example of how a usually successful professional responded to negative feedback. Consider the case of comedian Sarah Silverman, who is used to getting feedback and reviews calling her one of the funniest performers around. However, like most of us who get judged by others when we perform in public, we don't always hit the ball out of the park—ergo, my performance at the university seminar. In 2008, Silverman performed at the Hammersmith Apollo in London, in front of 3,500 people packing the theater who paid $100 or more for a performance that had been promoted for weeks. The only problem was, Silverman did between thirty-five and forty minutes of material, and when she announced the show was over, the crowd was in shock and started to boo.

Many were chanting that they wanted their money back. Others yelled, "You are over-hyped Sarah." To appease the unruly crowd giving her very negative feedback, Silverman reappeared on stage in her post-show slippers saying she didn't have any more material but she would be willing to do a Q&A. That quickly flopped, with more fans booing and many others leaving. One fan yelled out; "I've seen longer clips on YouTube." According to the BBC, Silverman got very defensive and yelled to the crowd to "go home" and then added an exclamation point by offering this gem: "F*** this." The video is available on YouTube.

According to London *Times* reviewer Dominic Maxwell, who was there for the performance, there was no excuse for Sarah Silverman's negative and defensive reaction to a crowd that was simply asking for more. Said Maxwell, "As Silverman stalked the stage, appearing to resent her crowd for wanting more, it was the eggiest end to a comedy show I've ever seen. . . . She blew it."[1]

The moral here isn't about comedy. It is about all of us as professionals under pressure who can be defensive and react negatively when we get feedback that hurts. Granted, criticism is hard to hear, but the best thing you can do is to take a breath and realize you can't argue or debate with someone who thinks you haven't gotten the job done. It could be an audience of 1,000 or your core colleagues in the workplace or a single client or key stakeholder. A leadership lesson: You are not going to convince everyone that you were great if they think you weren't, so stop trying. Your best bet as a leader, whether it is in business or any other arena, is to graciously accept the feedback even if you don't agree with it. Also, it wouldn't hurt to apologize for people's disappointment, or at least acknowledge that you understand their point of view.

Further, as a leader, when presenting in public, if you sense you are in fact losing the crowd, you have to step up your game. Simply put, when receiving negative feedback, you need to engage your audience on a different level. Add more passion. Give more of yourself. Become more personally involved. Work harder to connect with your audience and maybe, just maybe, they will appreciate the effort, even if your game is a little bit off. I know I have been there more than I'd like to admit. Defending yourself and resisting negative feedback only guarantees a bad outcome. Just ask the usually very funny Sarah Silverman, who owed her audience a lot more that night in 2008.

With this in mind, remember that when receiving feedback that is less than glowing, it is incumbent upon all of us as leaders to fight the urge to fight back. Of course, it is a defense mechanism, but the problem is that we don't take a closer look at our performance. The person providing the feedback isn't saying you are bad. They are just saying you could be better. Who among us can't improve? I know I can, which is why when I got past my initial defensiveness regarding the university seminar, I realized that some of the negative feedback the dean was sharing with me was valuable, and I've taken it into account in future seminars I've led.

The 360 Leadership Assessment Tool

Great leaders understand that receiving feedback shouldn't be done in a haphazard or less than strategic fashion. Of course, it needs to be done on a regular basis, and people around you need to feel comfortable sharing their honest assessment of your strengths as well as opportunities for you to improve. The best leaders proactively seek feedback from those around them in an organized manner. Consider what I call the "360 Leadership Assessment Tool," which can be an important way of providing valuable and direct feedback about a leader's performance.

The 360 tool, which is often confidential and seeks information from a leader's supervisors, direct reports, peers, and important external stakeholders (therefore the 360), is considered a *must* when it comes to finding out how well a leader is doing and what he or she can improve on. But just doing a 360 doesn't make it valuable in itself. In fact, it has the potential of confusing and sometimes frustrating a leader when he or she really doesn't understand the feedback or, worse, what behavior is supposed to change. It is the ability to engage in an honest, collegial, and supportive conversation, but most of all the opportunity to provide specific feedback that makes the 360 work. As leaders we must insist that the feedback we receive is tangible, concrete, and based on real-world situations.

In my work, I've seen HR consultants get caught up in delivering voluminous, color-coded 360 profiles with more charts and graphs than any one person can handle. But beyond the bells and whistles, here are some tangible ways to ensure that the 360 Leadership Assessment Tool works for you:

- Define your terms. It is not enough to say that a leader or any professional being evaluated must "take more responsibility." You must share specifically what you mean by that. For example: "Jim, we feel you need to take more responsibility when putting the team's meeting agenda together. Proactively, share your ideas as to what should be on that agenda at least a week before the meeting. When you do this, we get the benefit of your insight." The point is that until Jim understands exactly what is meant by taking on "more responsibility," he can interpret it in countless ways. As George Bernard Shaw is believed to have said, "The single biggest problem in communication is the illusion that it has taken place." A powerful leadership lesson is to assume there is a real possibility of misunderstanding until you clearly confirm that understanding has occurred.

- Meet face-to-face. As an employee's direct supervisor, it is important to set up a face-to-face meeting with someone who has just received his 360 assessment results. This is tricky, because the 360 is sometimes confidential, meaning the employee is not required to share it with anyone. Yet, if key aspects of it are not shared and explored further, improvement rarely takes place. The leader should proactively share with the employee the importance of agreeing on a performance improvement plan that can be measured over time. The leader can say, "Mary, what area of your 360 do you want to work on to improve?" Then together you can build a foundation of a coaching plan.

- Don't get caught up in the numbers. On a standard 360 assessment, an employee is asked to rate on a scale from 1 to 5 his performance in a certain area, for example, "Involves his staff in decisions that affect the team's performance." A score of 1 is pretty bad, and 5 is great. The problem is that people grade themselves and others using very different standards. A 3 to Jim may be a 5 to Mary. Organizational leaders must make it clear that the numbers can be and often are deceiving. Further, they must make it clear that it is the "360 narrative" that is most important. This narrative is in the form of open-ended comments communicated by workplace colleagues. For example: "Joan needs to improve her presentation skills" or "Bob needs to work on being a more engaged and present listener."
- Don't let the 360 be a once-a-year experience. A scaled-down version of it should be administered at the midyear point. The abbreviated 360 should focus on a team member's progress in specific areas identified as those that needed to be improved. If in fact an employee is making progress, it is critical that the team leader recognize and acknowledge such progress.

Organizations can spend millions of dollars on a 360 and other comprehensive employee review tools. But going through the motions and filling out the forms won't get the job done. Only through genuine human interaction that provides honest and sometimes hard-to-hear feedback can the 360 make a difference when it comes to improving the performance of a leader or any team member.

Being Defensive Leads to Bad Results: Meet Jane

A few months ago, I was working with an executive named Jane who was receiving feedback through the 360 Leadership Assessment Tool that asked the following two questions of colleagues who know her best: What are my three greatest qualities as a leader? What are three specific areas where I can improve? When done with an open mind and a spirit of wanting to get better, this exercise yields great results. However, in Jane's case, she was especially resistant to the feedback—a trait shown by many leaders.

Specifically, when Jane's executive assistant, Betty, said she could be condescending when giving directives or dealing with mistakes, Jane's response was, "Yes, but the problem with Betty is that I have to tell her the same thing 100 times before she gets it right." Jane was being defensive, so instead of receiving this valuable feedback and using this information to find ways to improve the way she interacts with Betty, she wanted me to understand that she had a perfectly good explanation for leading and interacting in this fashion.

As we proceeded through the results of her assessment, Jane continued to defend herself against any negative feedback until I finally asked her this question, "Jane, if this is how others perceive your leadership style, what's the downside to accepting it from your colleagues' perspective and trying to find a better way of getting your message across?" At that point, she stared at me, and it was clear that Jane had been stuck in this defensive-leadership mode for a very long time.

Jane is not alone. All of us have engaged in defensive leadership, but when we do, nothing good happens. So why not consider this more constructive (and yes, more challenging) approach the next time you receive feedback that's less than glowing:

- Don't just go with your first instinct. That may be appropriate in some professional arenas, but when it comes to this type of gut reaction in leadership, it is often bad advice. Many times, our first instinct is to be defensive, because defending ourselves is natural. Rather, take a breath and fight that urge to fight back. Instead of saying, "What you don't understand is . . . ," you could say, "Tell me more about what happens when I speak to you in that tone." Asking this question allows you to listen to the impact your leadership style has on others.
- Go into "solution mode." Ask yourself what you are really trying to accomplish here. Is it to win an argument or to explain why you are doing something? Or is it to get to a better place with someone who matters in your professional and personal

life? Being solution-oriented will change everything about the way you interact with others. It will cause you to say things like "Joe, what about if I were to. . . ." The idea is to propose to Joe a different style of communication to gauge how he would react to it.

- Consider the point of view of others; your approach may not be the only or best one. Accept that you are not perfect and that the other person giving you feedback has a perspective that can genuinely benefit you. Looking at things from the other person's point of view is one of the most valuable leadership lessons and will cause you to be less defensive. (The subject of empathy is explored in greater detail in chapter 5 of this book.)

Of course, all of this is easier said than done and, in the heat of the moment, is sometimes difficult to execute. But if you decide that being defensive as a leader has gotten in the way of your reaching your potential to date, why not try a different approach? What do you have to lose, other than lots of unnecessary frustration and anxiety?

11

Leadership Is *Very* Personal

There is no exact science to the art of leadership. People are moved and motivated by all kinds of people, events, and circumstances. A particularly effective and grounding leadership tool is the use of simple, yet profound, aphorisms or quotes. These aphorisms or quotes can come from business gurus, sports or spiritual figures, artists, or movies. (I am partial to the leadership lessons in *The Godfather* such as "Keep your friends close, but your enemies closer," which I discuss in chapter 21.) The key is that wherever they come from, these very sayings help us, particularly in troubling times when we as leaders feel frustrated, confused, or downright lost.

A longstanding saying or cliché that many take for granted can be turned on its head and challenged by a strong leader who lives it every day, as opposed to living in a world based in theory. Recently, my longtime friend and golf partner Nick Matarazzo, who is the CEO of Jumpstart Automotive Group, sent me an e-mail under the heading of: "It's not personal, it's just business."

To his credit, Nick, who has been leading people for over twenty-five years and deals in a highly competitive arena, challenged this saying with the following; "If one doesn't make it personal, then it's just about the money. That is a very shallow way to go through life. My clients know I care about their business. If their business does well, then they—as people—are successful. That is very personal. Leading is influencing and empowering others, and one needs compassion, vision, and insight to accomplish this. Trust me, this is highly personal."

Nick has it right. Of course business is personal; therefore, leadership is highly personal. It's personal because you are ultimately dealing with people. When someone gets fired because his boss says he is just not getting the job done, how can you expect the person not to take it personally? Someone's self-esteem is taking a hit. Take a look at Abraham Maslow's hierarchy of needs. I imagine you *could* say it's not personal. In theory, it's not personal when a business you poured your life savings into goes bankrupt, but when you are then unable to pay your mortgage or send your kids to college because of it, how can you say that's not personal?

When a leader acts in a neglectful or less than assertive fashion and fails to protect those he is responsible for, how can we say, "It's not personal, it's just business?" Consider the case of Newark Archbishop John Myers of the Catholic Church, who said on multiple occasions that he was unaware of, or that others beneath him were responsible for, the sexual molestation of children by priests who reported directly to Myers. Ask the parents of those children, who are now adults, if it was personal.

What about when a college basketball coach leaves a program to go to the pros after getting a multimillion-dollar contract offer. Ask the eighteen-year-old freshman and his parents whom that same coach visited and recruited six months earlier to come to the college with this promise—"I will take care of your son as if he were my own"—if it's not personal.

Or consider the young professional who spends years trying to make partner in a law or accounting firm by doing all that is asked of him, yet doesn't reach that goal in large part because the partner charged with the responsibility of mentoring, coaching, and developing him never really cared enough to invest the time and effort needed to help him reach his goal. Is this leadership failure personal or simply business?

Finally, when in a meeting a department head ridicules and insults a team member who has made her best effort on an important project by saying, "Jane, you are an embarrassment to our organization. I'm ashamed that you have the nerve to even present this report." Not personal? Really?

Leadership is personal because we care deeply about how we are treated as professionals and as people and we care about the products and services we provide to our customers. Leadership is personal because so much about who we are as people is connected to what we do in our business or professional lives.

On the positive side, when a teacher tries to connect with and help a struggling student by using a variety of engaging and creative teaching tools—is that not personal? When you work long hours over a weekend or late at night to solve a client's problem or to close a deal that helps pay your company's bills, and ultimately the salary and benefits of your employees, how can we say that this is "simply business"? It's not. Again, it's highly personal—because it's about people.

Similarly, consider what message is sent when a team leader takes the time and cares enough to understand what is going on with an employee's gravely ill parent or family member and asks, "What can I do to help?" or says, "I want you to know I understand that even though we take our work seriously, family always comes first. So, if you need to take some time to take care of things, all you have to do is ask."

What about a leader who has an extremely valuable employee who he knows is playing out of position or is simply in the wrong job given the employee's skills and talent. When that leader concludes that the employee's prospects would be better in another department or division of the organization or even another organization overall—and helps facilitate such a transition—how much of this is personal? I say a lot!

Finally, I was reminded of how personal business can be when I interviewed Vincent Curatola, a prominent cast member of *The*

Sopranos, following the death of James Gandolfini, the star of that HBO hit series. In our conversation, Curatola told me a touching and poignant story about how the cast of *The Sopranos* was negotiating for more money and when HBO resisted, Gandolfini personally interceded on behalf of his lesser known and much lesser paid cast members—something very few leading men or women would do—and said he wouldn't work unless they were in fact paid more. Further, Gandolfini gave hundreds of thousands of dollars from his own pocket to individual cast members in an effort to boost their salaries. Gandolfini would also consistently give cast members very special gifts to celebrate his success and the success of the series.

As Vincent Curatola told me this story about his late friend and colleague, his emotions and personal loss were evident. He was clearly moved not only by James Gandolfini's untimely death but by his personal and human connection with him. Was the way Gandolfini treated his castmates "just business"? Ask his former colleagues who still grieve his loss if they feel his friendship—and yes, his leadership—wasn't personal. Of course it was, and that's what made all the difference. Clearly leadership can be personal even though we must maintain a level of objectivity and clear thinking in our decision making.

"Hug" Your People: Show Them You Care

When I think of James Gandolfini and how he treated his cast mates on *The Sopranos*, it reminds me of my friend and colleague, Jack Mitchell, who has branded the concept of "hugging" in his two books, *Hug Your Customers: A Master of Customer Service Reveals His Secrets for Developing Long-Lasting Business Relationships and Customer Loyalty* as well as *Hug Your People: The Proven Way to Hire, Inspire, and Recognize Your Employees and Achieve Remarkable Results*. I've interviewed Jack several times on public television, talking about this whole "hugging" notion. What it really comes down to is showing people that you care—the people you work with as well those you serve as customers and clients.

A really big leadership lesson works the same way. As leaders, we need to "hug" more than we do. We need to proactively and consistently show those around us how much we care for them, not only as employees or as paying customers, but as people who are a big part of our success as leaders.

With this in mind, consider some of the actions that you can take as a leader to show those who matter how much you care, because in this arena, leadership is highly personal.

- Show your team you value work-life balance. I'm working on this book during the summer. The weather's been great, and I'm writing a lot down at the Jersey Shore. One of the things I've come to realize as a leader is that the people on our team who work hard every day really appreciate getting out early on Fridays, especially when the weather is particularly nice. Let's face it—work is never really slow, yet July and August are not nearly as hectic as other times of the year. So, as a leader, why not establish "summer hours," especially on Fridays or Mondays, so that your people can have a longer weekend to spend time with their family and do the things that they find personally rewarding? It may seem small, but this gesture will go a long way.
- Be aware of the "big things" going on in the lives of others. Very often, people on our team have personal situations that can be challenging and very difficult, such as an illness in the family or the loss of a loved one. Or, on a happier note, an employee might be especially proud of a child who's performing in an important play or recital. Leaders need to be aware of these circumstances, because while we may expect professionals to separate their personal lives from work, this is unrealistic on many levels when it comes to the really "big things." As the late Richard Carlson wrote in *Don't Sweat the Small Stuff*, leaders need to be aware, sensitive, and empathetic when it comes to the "big things" in the lives of those around us. Leaders must not only ask about how their people are doing, but genuinely care about how their people are doing. For example, if extra

time off is needed, don't hesitate to give it; ask if the employee in question wants to talk, and be sensitive to the workload you assign to him or her during this particular time.

- Support and encourage team members to further their education or seek professional development. Often, it takes a leader who truly understands how difficult it is to balance all of the competing demands on employees' lives to push and encourage employees to do the things that are necessary to advance their careers. Over the past decade, I've done a significant amount of leadership development and executive coaching work at CohnReznick, one of the largest accounting firms in the country. Some of the most successful leaders in the firm are the ones who have dedicated themselves to helping junior staff members and managers pass the all-important CPA exam. This is no easy task, and many professionals in the accounting world have had their careers thwarted because they have been unable to overcome this hurdle.

Further, great leaders understand that motivating their team members takes a lot more than simply telling them, "You need to pass your CPA exam" or every once in a while encouraging them to do so. What it really takes is sitting down with team members to find out what is standing in their way, what obstacles and challenges they are facing, and whether any of these obstacles have to do with time constraints arising from their work on current engagements with clients. Sometimes, it involves rearranging schedules and work assignments in the short term to give them the opportunity to study and focus on preparing for the exam, and checking in on a regular basis to ensure that this in fact is happening. If someone happens to fall short on one or more parts of the CPA exam, the exceptional leader steps in with positive words of encouragement and feedback on the need to stay the course and take the exam again. A lot of this is clearly about professional development, but it's also about a very personal commitment that the leader makes to other human beings to help them reach their professional potential. It can have a long-lasting impact on people's earning potential and quality of life, as well as their family situation and ultimate happiness.

Which part of this isn't "personal"? This leadership lesson does not only apply to leaders helping others pass the CPA exam. You could also encourage and support your colleagues, peers, or direct reports to pursue a particular academic or professional degree, attend a leadership development seminar, or participate in executive coaching to improve skills. Further, if you feel that someone's work-life balance needs an adjustment, encourage that person to take the necessary time off to do these things. The point is, great leaders understand the value of making a personal investment in their people. The payoff for both parties can be huge.

- Find common ground with clients and stakeholders. This is one of the biggest leadership lessons I share throughout this book, and when it comes to clients, a leader's job is to make sure that he or she develops the appropriate personal relationships with key stakeholders who have a direct impact on the organization's success. This often means spending time with these stakeholders in a variety of settings outside the workplace. Some of the most meaningful work a leader can do is over a breakfast, lunch, or dinner meeting, as people often feel especially comfortable and relaxed in this informal setting.

- Place a call, type an e-mail, or send a congratulatory note or card when something special happens for a colleague or client. Things happen in people's lives that matter, and when we work around colleagues for as much time as we do it's almost impossible not to know when these things happen. The question is, what does a really caring leader do in these situations? Does the leader say, "It's not my business because it has nothing to do with the workplace?" In the rare instance, this may be true. However, in the vast majority of cases, letting your people know that you are aware of what has occurred is the right thing to do—be it an especially positive event such as the birth of a child or one that is tragic, difficult, or challenging. It's the golden rule. It's simply about treating people the way any one of us would want to be treated if we were experiencing the same thing. This is basic common decency.

I have worked with many leaders who are tone-deaf in this area. Yet, the really good leaders understand the leadership lesson in all of this. While of course we *work* together, personal lives do matter, and letting people know that you care on a personal level, while not invading their privacy, is not only appropriate but often necessary.

As they would do with a team member or peer, smart leaders would also congratulate professional colleagues or stakeholders on an accomplishment (professional or personal) or even on the success of someone they care about, such as a spouse or child. One of my favorite clients, whom I've worked with for over a decade and who is an exceptional leader, recently traveled to Florida for his elderly mother's birthday but insisted that we take care of some important business over the phone while he was there. Both of us knew that it was very clear to me that it was his mother's birthday, so it felt totally natural for me to send an e-mail to him wishing his mom all the best on this special day. This gesture was personal because it mattered to him and because he and I have had countless conversations about our children, our parents, and our families for many years. Therefore, congratulating his mom just felt right.

That's the point about leadership often being very personal. It's about relationships and interacting with other people on a very human level, which was much of the theme of my second book, *Make the Connection*. Leaders who don't make that connection on a human and personal level, no matter how smart they are or think they are, will never truly succeed.

Know the Pulse of Your Team

We are all members of a team—whether that team is at our place of work as department members, in our homes as family members, in our communities, in our schools, or in our churches. At some point in our lives, we all combine our energy and skills with those of others to accomplish a common goal. On our various teams, the members may come from different backgrounds and different skill levels, and they may have different approaches to business and life, but still we come together to accomplish things that none of us can accomplish individually.

Team success depends on the quality of the personal relationships among the individual members of the team. The leader of a team must know the people on his or her team; the leader has to gain their trust and has to encourage them to trust each other. This takes time and a conscious effort on the team leader's part, but if he or she uses the right tools to build solid, trustworthy relationships among team members, the time and effort spent will be well worth it. The team leader needs to have a sense of who each team member is as a human being. One way to gain this information is through face-to-face, informal conversations. Occasionally having coffee or lunch with team members is a wise investment of time that will pay off down the line. Informal conversation gives the group leader the opportunity to find out what each person is looking for, what this person hopes to contribute to the team, and what kind of work style is best.

Ongoing, open, and honest conversations will also reveal personal life circumstances that need to be understood by the team leader and other team members. If a member of the team has a challenging situation at home involving an elderly parent, spouse, or a young child, everyone on the team should be sensitive to this. This doesn't mean the group leader should lower standards, but it will allow the leader to be sympathetic and empathetic to that person and make arrangements that will help him or her contribute to the team in a more optimal way. Sometimes, that might mean allowing someone to work from home for a while, or allowing someone to come in early and leave early. Team leaders need to be firm but flexible. It will also help other team members understand the bigger picture and the actions of the leader. How can you expect to get the most productive work out of people if you don't know what they're grappling with in other areas of life? Getting to know each team member is the first step toward creating a productive unit.

A few years ago, former Newark police director Garry McCarthy was reminded of this important lesson when a ceremony was held honoring several Newark police officers for their bravery on the job and only a couple of dozen of their colleagues showed up. It was embarrassing to the police department and sent a powerful message about how morale within the department was not where it should have been. Director McCarthy was clearly disappointed that officers didn't show up, telling a reporter for the *Star-Ledger*, "There are things I took for granted, and I'm finding out that I can't."[1]

One police officer said anonymously, "You're lucky to get guys to come to work when you are paying them. These are not happy cops that are out in the street."[2] Whether you are dealing with police officers, teachers, corporate managers, or employees, morale is a key to organizational success. So how *do* you keep people happy and productive, and how much of that has to do with great leadership? What do your employees want and need to stay motivated in these challenging times and what can you as a leader do to make a difference and, once again, truly get to know your team members and what makes them tick? Here are some tangible tips and tools that belong in your leadership tool kit:

- Take the time to check in with your people and find out how they are feeling about what they are doing. Sometimes employees have to do certain jobs that they don't want to do but are necessary. However, that doesn't mean that the way the job is done can't be changed or improved. Seek out your employees' thoughts on finding a new way of doing old tasks, for example: "Jane, what exactly would you change to get job X done in a more efficient or effective manner?" The more input Jane has into the way she does her job, the more motivated she is likely to be.
- Go out of your way to catch employees doing something right. This often doesn't come naturally to managers. Leaders have to really look for it and want to see it. It is so easy to

be blinded by people falling short or not meeting our expectations as a manager that we miss when they get it right. Do look for employee successes and when you find one, immediately let the employee know exactly how much you personally appreciate it and how the organization benefits from his or her efforts. For example: "Jim, I can't thank you enough for the job you did yesterday at the meeting. Your contribution helped us solve a nagging problem and will save the company a lot of money. We all appreciate it." Jim will feel on top of the world and will be motivated to do more and take risks, ultimately making a big difference in the organization. It will also send a message to fellow employees.

- *Don't* take your people for granted because they are currently doing a good job. In a marriage, if you simply assume everything is fine, it doesn't mean it is going to stay that way. You have to keep investing in the relationship without taking each other for granted. The same thing is true with employees. In the workplace, employees' attitudes change, even in our best and most productive people.

- *Don't* avoid dealing with the difficult employee who just doesn't seem to get it right. Many managers avoid confrontation, yet by not addressing this difficult employee, leaders communicate a powerful message that the status quo is acceptable when that's not the case. Of course, it is easier to turn a blind eye, but this comes at a hefty price. Don't avoid your "problem people," because they will only become bigger problems later.

- Establish trust among team members by creating opportunities to build personal relationships. You can't force team members to like each other or to be friends, nor should you even try. But truly getting to know your people will also present the possibility of putting them in situations where they can interact, connect, and find common ground with their colleagues in a way they wouldn't be able to do if you as a leader weren't aware enough to create such a positive and collaborative environment.

- Share the spotlight by encouraging team members to voice their opinions. Allow team members to make presentations both internally and externally; in fact, don't only allow it, but encourage it, report it, and reward it. Just because you may be the official leader of a team, or even the CEO, doesn't mean you should be doing all the talking. In fact, when you do this you send the message to your team that you believe you are the only one that has something to say. Plus, you do in fact lose touch with team members because they're convinced you have no confidence in them and their abilities.
- Don't make every decision. Rather, let others make some important decisions. Challenge team members to find the solution on their own with difficult problems and questions. Your objective is not only to get them to think for themselves but also to have them identify options and alternatives that you as a leader may not have thought of. In the process you will not only engage team members and motivate them, you will also get to know them better—including the way they think or don't think about strategic issues and decision making.
- Expect mistakes. It's part of the learning process. It's not the fact that mistakes happen that is the problem. It's what happens or doesn't happen when mistakes occur that is critical. Many leaders focus on either blaming or blasting their people, while others are so afraid of or averse to confronting the situation that they simply let mistakes go. They don't even deal with it, which is even worse than being the "blamer in chief," because the team member has no chance to learn or grow from the experience by understanding what he or she did wrong and, more importantly, what he or she can do to improve in the future. Really smart leaders see mistakes by team members as nothing more than an opportunity to teach. It is also, once again, a great opportunity to get to know your people in ways that you would never be able to if these mistakes weren't made.

Consider what former New York Jets football coach Rex Ryan had to say after his team's disappointing end to the 2011 season.

"Normally, I'm a guy that really has the pulse of his team. . . . I don't think I had the pulse of our team the way I [have] in the past. When I met with players [yesterday], that became clear to me."[3] Forget about football. What Rex Ryan was saying as a leader is one of the most candid and embarrassing things one can say in public— losing the "pulse" of your team. How does that happen? How do you *not* know that there is dissension and divisiveness within your team, when it is so publicly apparent? And isn't this in many ways a "personal" leadership failure? I would take it that way.

What is so ironic about what Coach Ryan said is that the person on the team who was most publicly disengaged and divisive, as the Jets were scrambling in the last game of the season, was wide receiver Santonio Holmes. Why is this significant? Because it was Holmes who was wearing an oversized letter C on his jersey, designating him as team captain. We are talking about the leader on the field. Rex Ryan, as the ultimate leader of his team, decided that his surrogate on the field would be Holmes—a guy who was relegated to the sidelines for constant arguing and complaining with other teammates because he wasn't getting the ball enough.

What's worse is that Holmes's antics were nothing new. Jets fans witnessed them in the first month of the season, during which he had complained in the media and was fighting with other team members. As a leader, Rex Ryan had to know that. If he *did* know and didn't do anything, that's bad enough. But to say, after an entire season, that you didn't have the "pulse" of the team? That's really bad. A great leader must put the right people in key positions.

What's so disappointing about Ryan's performance as a leader is that I had always been a fan of his passion and enthusiasm in the way he publicly advocates on behalf of his team. Yes, Rex Ryan moved on from the Jets after getting fired (and became the coach of the Buffalo Bills), but throughout his entire coaching career he has exuded confidence, predicting a Super Bowl win and other accomplishments. He has inspired and motivated his players, which is one of the most important things any coach, leader, or manager can achieve. But a leader's job entails more than that, because when things go wrong, a great leader must step up and confront those problems head-on. He *must* have the pulse of his team, particularly when that pulse is beating out of control, as opposed to simply simmering under the surface.

Sometimes, it is too uncomfortable for us, as leaders, to face serious problems in our organization. However, when we avoid them, inevitably these problems publicly explode and the situation is more difficult and complicated to address. So what happened in the case of the Jets? Rex Ryan held a post-season press conference in which he broke down, and explained his emotional reaction this way: "It's hurtful. I'm extremely prideful. I want to be the best. I want to win. Sometimes it comes out like that." Leadership is not personal? Really?

What is the bottom line? Leading with emotion and passion is essential for any great leader, but losing the pulse of your team negates all of that. There is a huge lesson for the rest of us in listening to Coach Ryan's 2011 post-season analysis of what went wrong for the Jets. All of us must monitor the pulse of our team and our people. Achieving this often requires connecting on a personal level and maintaining a very personal relationship with our team members on a consistent basis. It's a critical responsibility that all of us in leadership positions must think about every day. Otherwise, we pay a hefty price.

Leading a team, being part of a team, winning together, losing together, growing together, sharing together, being together can be one of the most rewarding, fulfilling, and spiritually enriching experiences in your life. That's what it has been for me.

12

It's a Matter of Trust

I recently had the honor of emceeing the CohnReznick Foundation's 24th Annual Charity Golf Invitational, which raised more than $150,000 for two extraordinary organizations—the Special Operations Warrior Foundation (SOWF) and the Joe Torre Safe at Home Foundation. At this event, I was fortunate enough to speak with Joe Torre, the former Yankees manager and Hall of Famer, for a public television interview, in which he spoke openly about his early life, his family, his career as the manager of the Yankees, how he ultimately came to found the Joe Torre Safe at Home Foundation, and the importance of making a difference in the lives of others. During our interview, I had the opportunity to ask Torre about the greatest leadership lesson he has learned in baseball and in life. He responded, "Trust. I managed for almost thirty years and over this time I realized that you can employ all the strategy that you want. Yet, when it comes to the players that you're asking to commit to what you're trying to do and what you're trying to teach, the thing is that they have blood running through their veins. You need to have an understanding of each and every one of them. You can't treat them all the same.

My one goal is you have to treat them all fairly. You have to establish trust."

Joe Torre's best-selling book on leadership, *Ground Rules for Winners*, has influenced me greatly, and his words offer a powerful lesson to all of us. Without trust you can't lead. It's that simple—if your people don't trust you, they won't follow you. They won't believe you, and they likely won't give you the benefit of the doubt. It's hard enough to lead successfully when times are good, but when times get challenging, difficult, uncertain, or even scary, a leader has absolutely no chance of succeeding and getting others to stay on board and remain loyal if he or she has not established trust. I've seen it countless times in organizations in which the leadership team hasn't been upfront in sharing important information with team members about things that are happening within the organization. As a result, these leaders have failed to build trust with employees over an extended period of time. So ask yourself what happens when times get tough? Revenues are down, some big clients are lost, there's a change at the top—one of the many "peaks and valleys" of running an organization. You know what happens, some of the best people on the team head for the exit. They leave. They quit. And when pressed as to why, a significant part of the reason often comes down to a lack of trust in the leader of the organization.

Yet, trust is a very complex thing. It's so hard to achieve but so easy to lose, and once you lose it, it seems so hard to get back. Leadership and trust is kind of like a marriage, when you think about it. For husband and wife, trust is the absolute core of that relationship, and when that trust is lost over an affair, a lie about something really important, a betrayal that seems unforgivable, what happens to that trust? And how hard is it to get back? Ultimately, what happens to that marriage, and what are the chances of that marriage succeeding? Is it that much different when it comes to the relationships leaders have with their people? But how exactly do leaders lose the trust of people around them? There are so many ways. Let's consider a few:

- Being self-centered and selfish. That's right. Money is tight. Some people are let go. Others are asked to take a pay cut, and what does the leader do? He takes a fat bonus. He makes sure he takes care of himself and his family financially. Once this is done, why would the people in the organization trust this leader regarding anything else, and why would they follow him into the line of fire? Would you? I know I wouldn't.

- Throwing a team member under the bus when the proverbial "@$%! hits the fan" or things go wrong. A lesson in leadership I write about extensively in chapter 19 explains that great leaders step up and take responsibility when things go wrong. One of the quickest ways for a leader to lose trust is to decide he's going to blame someone on the team instead of stepping up. For the person being thrown under the bus, all trust in that leader often goes out the window. Once again, why would others put their necks on the line for such a leader if, in fact, tire marks are fresh on the scapegoat, courtesy of the cowardly leader?

- Refusing to share credit. The opposite of throwing someone under the bus on the team is taking all of the credit for oneself. Too many leaders think, because they hold the top position in the organization, it is their job to have their name on every report and their right to get credit for everything within the organization. This couldn't be further from the truth. One of the fastest ways to lose trust is to not spread credit around. What makes a leader think that other people don't want to be recognized in the same way that he or she does? They do. So a leader who refuses to share credit—be it out of insecurity or a sense of misplaced narcissism—will once again lose the trust of team members who have no desire to see the leader succeed, because clearly he or she has no interest in the success of anyone else.

- Not sharing information about an important or sensitive organizational issue. Look, let's face it, mergers and acquisitions and organizational restructuring are more the norm than the exception these days. If a leader is actively pursuing a sale of the company or another major organization change but consistently tells team members, "The status quo is our plan," how could that leader expect to maintain the trust of others when something very different occurs in the future? Of course, I understand that not everything can be shared due to sensitive legal issues involving business transactions, but for a leader, telling outright lies to employees should never be an option when there are so many other ways to frame and position the details in order to simply let people know that the status quo is *not* the game plan. Promising one thing and doing another is a recipe for disaster and a surefire way to lose the trust of those around you.

This leadership lesson does not only apply to significant organizational changes. A truly great leader commits to telling the truth and to being upfront with his employees at all times possible. The alternative never works out well. For example, I've worked with many leaders who have promised individual employees a bonus, or a promotion, or a new position and then wound up doing something very different. Of course, sometimes things change, but when you refuse to acknowledge having made such a commitment and then breaking it, how can you expect the other person to continue to trust your word in the future? Further, what do you think is going to happen when others in the organization inevitably hear about such a story? Of course, the others are going to wonder if they can trust your word, and for good reason. Once again, I know I would have doubts. This concept brings me to my next point.

- Failing to be upfront and avoiding difficult conversations when the situation changes. Because circumstances can change so rapidly in our organizations and in life, an important lesson in leadership is to confront these difficult conversations directly. Avoiding them, particularly regarding the scenarios described in the bullet point above, only guarantees a build up of distrust and resentment. While having such difficult conversations may result in anger and disappointment, the people on the other end can't say you weren't forthright and honest about the situation, even if they are unhappy about the outcome. Smart leaders understand that by making sure these difficult conversations take place, as painful as they may be, they increase the odds of maintaining trust even if their people aren't happy with them or with how things turn out.

- Refusing to listen and being stubborn about your point of view. Want to lose the trust of your people? Then insist that you are right all of the time. Some of the worst leaders confuse stubbornness with being principled. If you want to lose the trust of the people around you, make sure your ideas are the only ones being heard—not listening to your team and their ideas will do the trick.

These are just some of the ways that leaders can lose the trust of those around them. Conversely, trust is something leaders need to work at every day. The following are some of the keys to building trust—a virtue that should never be taken for granted:

- Put others before yourself—not just as a leader but as a person. For example, during tough economic times for an organization, a CEO may take a pay cut—a major pay cut—in order to ensure that people's jobs will be saved or other worthy employees will get well-deserved raises. This builds trust in where the leader is coming from. However, few leaders are willing to do this, which is why it means so much when it does happen. In chapter 11, I discuss the story of the late James Gandolfini of *The Sopranos* who demonstrated this lesson in leadership when he refused to sign his deal with HBO until his fellow cast mates received significant pay hikes. Why? Because he deeply believed that as an ensemble cast they were being underpaid and underappreciated, and as a leader he knew it wouldn't be right to look out only for himself. In my conversations on PBS with *Sopranos* cast members Steve Schirripa, Dan Grimaldi, and Federico Castelluccio, all of them talked about the love, affection, and respect they felt for Gandolfini. Most of this came from the fact that they trusted that he had their back and that he had their best interests at heart. He was looking out for them and not simply making sure he got his own at whatever expense.

When a leader does this—be it on a hit TV series, on a sports team, or in a corporate setting—the payoff is huge because the trust factor is so high. So what do leaders receive in return as a payoff when such trust is established? Very often, those around such leaders will work harder and longer to achieve a particular goal. When things get tough and the chips are down for these leaders, their colleagues often are ready to offer support on many levels while others are abandoning ship. Further, these leaders who have built trust wind up getting more benefit of the doubt when they have to make tough or unpopular decisions about personnel or budget. There are no guarantees, but the odds are weighted in the leader's favor when the level of trust is so high.

- Simply do the right thing even when the easier option is obvious. For leaders, doing the right thing often involves difficult ethical or moral choices. These choices may be deeply unpopular with the people who are affected, but those closest to the situation will know that the leader did what had to be done to maintain the integrity of the organization and its mission. Very often, leaders are faced with difficult ethical and moral dilemmas in which they know what the right decision is, but financial considerations that impact the bottom line make those decisions more complicated. I'm not saying these choices are easy, but leaders in any arena who hope to maintain the trust of those around them must simply draw an ethical line and must not allow this line to move, out of expediency or because "we simply need the money." This leadership dilemma plays out every day not just in the world of public broadcasting, which I know very well, but in education and healthcare, in pharmaceutical sciences and finance. Your people have to believe that by and large they trust you to make ethical decisions that won't hurt innocent people. Consider the case of BP and its involvement in the disastrous oil spills in 2010, which devastated the Gulf Coast. Ask yourself, "Did the leaders of BP really not know the decisions they made in handling the spills were terribly risky and had the potential of imploding and ultimately wreaking the devastation it did?" Of course they did, but corporate profits mattered more. So how could they be trusted not just by employees of BP but by outside stakeholders and shareholders who trusted BP leaders to balance corporate profit with the larger public good? Leaders who throw caution to the wind and say "To hell with the public good, as long as we're making money" don't realize that they lose the trust of those around them—and when that happens, they fail to function effectively as leaders any longer.

• Be committed to the cause. Dr. Martin Luther King Jr. and Abraham Lincoln, among others, were genuinely committed to their causes, not just with words and speeches, but with sacrifice on a level that most of us find hard to comprehend. Growing up as a Catholic, reading and studying about how Jesus led others and ultimately died on the cross at thirty-three years old—always made me ask this question, "What kind of person would give up his life at thirty-three so that others could be given so much in return?" Now, this isn't a religious debate, and it doesn't really matter whether you are Catholic or not. Yet, the principle of self-sacrifice remains. When Dr. King spoke at the Mason Temple in Memphis, Tennessee, the night before he was assassinated, he said, "I've been to the mountain top" and "I'm not fearing any man." He also said he'd like to "live a long life" because "longevity has its place." However, he also made it clear that he was prepared to die for the cause of civil rights. King knew that there were many who wanted to do harm to him or likely kill him, but it didn't stop him from moving forward, seeking out and leading the cause of civil rights. He didn't back off, and he didn't parse his words. And, ultimately, at the age of thirty-nine, standing on that balcony at the Lorraine Motel in Memphis, he was assassinated.

Dr. Martin Luther King Jr. died committed to his cause. How could you separate what Dr. King did from the success of the civil rights movement—not just how he lived his life but also how he was prepared to die in leading this critical movement? His people trusted him because they knew he was courageous enough to put his life on the line. So they marched from Selma to Montgomery, Alabama, for the right to vote, only to be beaten by the police with clubs and attacked by vicious police dogs. They knew it would likely happen—there was blood everywhere. Women and children were seriously hurt and left lying on the ground, but who was in the front line leading that march in Selma? Bloodied and battered from a police baton, none other than Dr. King. It was only a precursor to his assassination.

Leaders who are willing to put their lives on the line and stand in front of those who follow them in the trenches build up extraordinary levels of trust. This kind of trust often inspires others to fight harder and longer for the cause. How many of us can really say that, as leaders, we are even close to being that courageous or committed to put our lives on the line for something we believe in? Not many, which makes the leaders I described here prime examples of a lesson in leadership we can all learn from, even if we can't reach their level of greatness.

13

Pumping Up Your People

For any leader, motivating and engaging your people, regardless of the arena, is always a challenge. Leaders often think motivating the people within the organization comes down to making a "rah-rah" speech or being a consummate cheerleader. Yes, part of your job as a leader is to do these things at certain moments, but if they're done in the absence of real substance, your words will likely fall on deaf ears. Your people don't want empty words; they want you to create a workplace environment that is rewarding, challenging, and inspiring. Yes, it's work, but employees want to have some *fun* while working or at least do so in a collegial, supportive, and enjoyable environment. Will their jobs be stressful at times? Of course. That's the nature of working under deadlines with a lot at stake, especially in a competitive environment where your excellence—in performance as well as execution—can be the difference between success and failure, not to mention staying in business or going belly up. Really good leaders consider all of this and, by using a range of leadership tools and conducting themselves in a certain way, are able to develop, motivate, and pump their people up to perform at their best.

With this goal in mind, consider the following leadership lessons, which will go a long way in motivating, engaging, and pumping up your people, particularly when it comes to getting through those especially difficult times:

- Hire people who exhibit a high level of energy, passion, and enthusiasm. Right off the bat, these characteristics will increase the odds that your employees will be more responsive to the challenge of new opportunities and will fit into the culture you are trying to build. There's no guarantee this will happen, but too often organizations hire the wrong people who look good on paper in terms of skills but don't have that special something—wanting to go beyond the job requirements to take more risks and responsibilities. It's important to find people who will step up when challenges arise, and who want to understand the organizational mission and how they can contribute to it. These special people are hard to find, but when you do, the payoff is huge.

- Create a mentoring and coaching culture. One of the keys to creating an engaged and supportive culture is to invest early in your people and not assume that just because they are talented, they will go the extra yard for the organization. This only happens in organizations where key leaders are consistently identifying those with the potential to grow. One of the ways I advocate building a coaching culture is by assigning individual team members as mentors to less experienced employees. Challenge them to develop their mentees into "future leaders" in the organization and hold them accountable over time. Through this approach, team players will feel responsible, not just for their own performance, but for the performance of others. Nothing motivates people more than helping colleagues develop their potential. It is exciting and exhilarating, but it doesn't happen by osmosis. It has to be organized and structured, and you need to select and coach the right people as mentors. The great leaders know this.

- Give employees challenging responsibilities that test their leadership potential. Expect more from your people than they expect from themselves. Great leaders push their people. They are constantly being creative by coming up with new projects and assignments that may make team members a little bit uneasy, but at the same time drive them to get outside of their comfort zone and achieve great things. This approach will definitely keep your people engaged.

  For example, consider the many highly entrepreneurial companies that have created spinoffs or subsidiaries lead by their most talented people. One of these companies is Zingerman's Deli in Ann Arbor, Michigan, which created nine businesses over thirty years and went from $5 million in annual sales to over $50 million during that time.[1] One of the keys to its success was not only to allow its people to identify new business lines but to let those same people step up and run those businesses. Some of the businesses succeeded wildly, while others didn't. But the key was to create the opportunity for those with the most entrepreneurial spirit to show their stuff after they had been given the necessary training.
- Lead interactive and goal-oriented meetings that force active employee participation. When you do this, team members get caught up in the spirit of accomplishing your organization's goals, and they can truly connect with your passion and enthusiasm. It is contagious in a positive way. The opposite approach will cause team members to become disengaged and unmotivated.
- Assign team members to lead certain meetings with clear goals and outcomes. Prior to those meetings, give other team members specific assignments that they must complete and come prepared ready to discuss. Smart leaders know they must give up the reins every once in a while to talented team members. As a result, these employees will become motivated to work harder and contribute more to the organization.
- Encourage team members to make presentations both internally and externally on important topics that they know well.

This may make some team members uncomfortable, if they find speaking in public to be nerve-wracking and anxiety-producing. But with the proper coaching and training, these same employees can make great strides in their presentation skills. Experiencing this improvement is extremely motivating, which will cause these same employees to want to get better by working harder in this area. Conversely, keeping your people within their comfort zone guarantees they will become stagnant and bored. Great leaders know that to grow, you have to get comfortable with being uncomfortable.

• Take team members to high-level meetings outside the office, which will expose them to challenging situations and important stakeholders. Then, be sure to debrief them afterward to find out what they took away from the experience. Involving team members in important meetings will help them feel a part of something special, something bigger. The stakes will be higher, and they will feel more important to the organization. This will cause them to be more motivated and engaged. Continue to show an ongoing interest in teaching, coaching and mentoring, which are the pinnacles of employee development. Showing that you care about an employee may be the ultimate motivator.

The key here is that there are many ways to motivate and engage your employees. As a leader, you must put in the time and the effort to understand what really pumps up your people and then commit yourself to work at doing so every day. As I discuss in chapter 18 of this book, truly exceptional leaders never stop learning, and one of the things I've learned after two decades of writing, teaching, and talking about leadership is that some of the best lessons can come from the most unlikely sources. When people talk about great leaders, they often reference corporate giants, historical political figures like Lincoln, or the Vince Lombardis of the sports world. But consider the following case of Dewey Finn, played by the over-the-top comedic actor Jack Black in the hit movie *School of Rock*. I use a scene from this movie in my leadership seminars in which Jack Black's character, an unlikely leader, motivates a group of young students in a variety of ways, which we can all add to our leadership tool kit.

Out-of-the-Box Leadership from Jack Black

In the movie *School of Rock*, the historically lazy and underachieving Dewey, played by Jack Black, had been obsessed with the idea of putting together a rock band that would compete in the local "Battle of the Bands." Although his passion was clear, Dewey was thrown out of his original band for not being a team player, not to mention selfish and narcissistic. He was clearly no leader. Later, Dewey takes a job as a substitute teacher (by stealing his friend Ned Schneebly's name and identity) in order to raise enough money to create his own band and enter the competition.

As a fake substitute teacher, Dewey was apathetic, uninspiring, and simply sat in front of the class reading comic books while students sat at their desks bored to tears. This went on for weeks, until one day Dewey saw his students practicing in a classical music class. While many of the students were musically talented, they seemed bored by the music class and the way it was being taught and led. Then, it hit him like a lightning bolt. "Mr. S," as his students called him, decided to create a "class project" in which his students would comprise the band that would compete with him in the upcoming Battle of the Bands he had been obsessing over for so long.

Immediately, he went to work, passionately teaching, mentoring, and yes, leading the students, not only showing them how to play "Smoke on the Water" by Deep Purple, but getting them excited about doing so. If you've never seen the movie, do yourself a favor and rent it. Mr. S does a variety of things to demonstrate exceptional leadership, which are all about the way he motivates and inspires the students to want to be a part of something meaningful—something fun. He praises some of the quietest kids, and he shows others how to play instruments they've never even tried to play before—doing all this with great enthusiasm, passion, and a smile on his face.

In one telling scene, he informs the kids selected to be in the band that they are ready to compete and that the rest of them, who were not selected for the band, should sit back and "enjoy the magic of rock." Yet, just then, one of the students who was a quiet spectator asked, "So, you mean we are not in the band?" Instinctively, Mr. S—who has become an engaged and insightful leader—replies, "Just because you are not in the band, doesn't mean you are not *in* the band. We need backup singers . . . who can sing?" A few kids raise their hands. Many are in fact exceptional singers while others are just okay, but all of them get encouragement from their teacher. Finally, he says, "We are going to find a job for everyone, because all of you are going to be in the band."

One of the biggest leadership lessons in *School of Rock* is realizing that all of us, whether we are a ten-year-old kid or forty-five-year-old middle manager, want to "be in the band." Not necessarily in an actual band, but we all want to be part of something bigger than ourselves. Even those who are sitting on the sidelines in offices everywhere still want to "be in the band," but they need to be invited to do so in a supportive and enthusiastic fashion. Great leaders understand that even those who don't speak up and volunteer on a regular basis for team projects or assignments need to be encouraged—and sometimes challenged—to step up and participate and become "part of the band."

Further, an important lesson to remember is that sometimes it is *your* responsibility as the leader not just to be responsive to team members who desire to actively participate but to proactively call them out—even if they don't ask or if they have said they are uncomfortable participating or leading a team project. Great leaders create a safe environment for team members to take risks and try new things. This approach will motivate your people, engage them, and yes, pump them up! This leadership approach also reminds team members that everyone has the potential to actually lead and not just participate. The first step is making sure you create a place "in the band" for all of your people—the way Jack Black's Mr. S did in *School of Rock*.

This leadership skill is all about knowing your people and what motivates them as individuals, including the need to be a part of something, be it a band or a new team within the organization taking on a daunting challenge. It all comes down to communicating and connecting with people on a deeper, more personal level and, when offering challenges, following up with encouragement and support. That's what exceptional teachers do, which is very similar to what the best leaders do. Pretty simple, isn't it?

14

Getting the Wrong People
Off the Bus

I was talking the other day to a client who heads up a major corporation. This company has been successful in not just recruiting but retaining clients and customers. Its fees are relatively high, but the service it offers is first rate. For years, the CEO of the company had told me that its executives were considering reducing the workforce but decided against it, because times were good and they had gotten what he called "fat and happy." The people he wanted to let go were underachievers—people who just weren't producing or "carrying their weight." In fact, there was a list of employees, including many in top leadership positions, whose names came up over and over again as people who were pulling the organization down. However, in an effort to "maintain morale" and send a message that "things were good," nothing was done and these unproductive employees stayed on the payroll. Don't rock the boat, right?

Yet, after the fall of 2008, everything changed. The company lost numerous clients and revenues dipped. The leadership of the company got nervous and decided after the first of the year it was finally time to act. Soon after, they decided they were going to let nearly a hundred people go. That's right, these were the same unproductive employees whose names were on that list for years. It was done quickly and efficiently, and according to the CEO, "There wasn't a single protest or objection from any executive or manager to any one of the names." The CEO remarked, "We are not going to miss a beat because these people are gone." Yet, he added, "But we made a mistake. We should have done this a couple of years ago, but we avoided it. At the time, we were trying to be compassionate to these people and their families, but we now realize we didn't do anyone a favor, given the current economy with so few jobs out there."

So there you have it. This story could be retold in organizations everywhere across America. It's one of the most difficult lessons involving leadership. It is one of the hardest messages to deliver, but it has to be done and there is no right time to do it. Letting someone go who either is not performing after continual coaching and training or has a negative attitude and is always badmouthing the organization is something that must be done. I'm talking about people who do the bare minimum or won't pitch in when the organization needs them, people who complain on a regular basis and create a negative mood and environment by the way they conduct and carry themselves. I hate to use this expression, but they often become a "cancer" within the organization.

Yet, often, in an effort to be compassionate, many leaders allow unproductive and negative employees to stay on the payroll—or the proverbial "bus" as Jim Collins describes in his book, *Good to Great.*[1] Consider the message leaders send when they do this, not only to those unproductive and negative people who stay, but to all those high producers and positive employees who are left picking up the slack and feeling resentful. The company is saying it doesn't matter how hard you work or how much value you bring with your "what can I do to help our team succeed" attitude because there are no consequences for not getting the job done or continuing to be a "Debbie Downer" or "Mediocre Mike" in the workplace. So why, then, should a top-notch employee keep putting in so much effort for an organization that doesn't treat him any differently from the guy down the hall who has been dogging it or complaining for years?

Despite all of the reasons to let go of certain people described in this chapter, I have lost count of the number of clients in leadership positions who have delayed doing so, and have sometimes outright refused to confront this unacceptable situation directly over the years. Explanations given by these leaders go well beyond some sense of compassion or empathy for a poorly performing or negative employee. Some of these leaders have told me how long they have known or worked with a particular employee, or how they have socialized or become friendly with them.

For example, one leader told me about a manager who was leading an important department within his organization that he knew had been underperforming for years: "I've known Bob for over fifteen years. I've been to his family parties. I went to his son's bar mitzvah. We even went on a vacation cruise with our wives and a bunch of other people a few years ago. But he is absolutely terrible as a manager of this department." When I pressed this leader about the impact of keeping Bob "on the bus," his expression turned sour and he cried, "He's killing us and everyone knows it! My board is not happy with me. They don't know why I haven't let him go. What's worse is that Bob has really poor people skills, and some of our most talented people, who could really help that department, just won't work with him." As I write this chapter, this client has yet to confront the "Bob situation" head-on. It's serious. He hasn't been able to bring himself to do what a good leader must do when a key team member is consistently hurting the organization as well as the bottom line.

A bit of self-disclosure is important right here. Even though I have coached and consulted dozens of leaders in this particular area, there have been times when I have fallen short as the leader and CEO of my own organization, a television production company affiliated with public broadcasting. I am ultimately responsible for all of my employees. Yet, for years, after I personally recruited and hired a key member onto our senior team, I failed to do what I should have done—what I had coached others to do when it came to getting someone "off the bus." All seemed fine with this VP for the first year or so. At first, when a problem arose I would simply talk things through with him. Then, I became increasingly frustrated. I found myself not only complaining but actually doing key aspects of his job, which made me more frustrated and resentful. It soon became clear that no matter how many times this team member missed deadlines, didn't follow up on important projects, and had me micromanaging his performance—thing weren't getting any better. I complained about the situation to my wife, my closest friends, and to senior members of our team. But as a leader, I was allowing this situation to manage me and not the other way around. I was feeling sorry for myself: "Why can't he just do his job?" It made me angry and overly edgy.

So, a couple of years into this very unhealthy situation, I suggested to two of my most senior managers that we should do something about it. One of the managers, who was especially close to the VP, resisted. The other top manager said I had to make the call on my own but made it clear that we had a small, close-knit staff and that letting the VP go would have a negative impact on morale. So once again, I punted. I passed. I did nothing, which is sometimes one of the worst decisions a leader can make. I was a weak leader. A major lesson in leadership is that doing nothing is sometimes anything but neutral or benign. I failed to do the job that I was being paid to do as CEO. I was not only letting down the members of my team, whether they would have liked my decision or not, but I was also letting down our key stakeholders as well as my board of trustees.

The organization was clearly not reaching its potential in key areas because of this situation, and I knew it better than anyone else. I had become resigned to the situation but continued to be unhappy about it. All the while, I was coaching others to do what I wasn't doing myself. But then, one day, the VP called me to say he had something "very important but very difficult to tell me." In fact, he told me—after much internal debate—that he had decided to take another job. Of course, I wished him nothing but the best in his new professional endeavor. Privately, I did a happy dance and immediately called my wife to tell her the news. She said, "You're off the hook, but not because of anything you did. . . . You caught a break, now do something with it."

Immediately, I began to think of the kind of person our organization needed in this critical position. A talented, committed professional who would add great value to our team. In fact, after a few months of interviews, that's exactly who we found. I can't tell you the impact it's had. As an organization we are much more productive. The VP hired is infinitely more creative, proactive, entrepreneurial, and hardworking. She is a leader. She's invested and she challenges me every day to be better at what I do. We collaborate consistently and I rarely, if ever, micromanage in her area. When I do, she is totally open to the feedback unless she has strong disagreements, which she cares enough to share with me. Yet, like so many leaders who have been in a similar position, I realize that I can't get back the time when I knew I should have escorted a key employee who was performing poorly off the bus that I was driving.

Talk about a leadership lesson. Trust me, I learned a big one. As Jim Collins says in *Good to Great*: "The executives who ignited the [organizational] transformations from good to great did not first figure out where to drive the bus and then get people to take it there. No, they FIRST got the right people on the bus (and the wrong people off the bus) and THEN figured out where to drive it. They said, in essence, 'Look, I don't really know where we should take this bus. But I know this much: If we get the right people on the bus, the right people in the right seats, and the wrong people off the bus, then we'll figure out how to take it someplace great.'"[2]

The truly exceptional leader understands that. "If you have the right people on the bus, the problem of how to motivate and manage people largely goes away. The right people don't need to be tightly managed or fired up; they will be self-motivated by the inner drive to produce the best results and to be part of creating something great. If you have the wrong people, it doesn't matter whether you discover the right direction; you still won't have a great company. Great vision without great people is irrelevant."[3]

Finally, I am not advocating that leaders indiscriminately look for people to fire and put on the unemployment line in these difficult economic times. The leadership lesson in this chapter isn't about demonstrating how tough or aggressive you are for the sake of it. Rather, the leadership lesson is about doing what is difficult but necessary—getting rid of the people in your organization who are not contributing to the team's success. It has nothing to do with their being bad people. In fact, many times, poor performers can be really nice and pleasant. But nice and pleasant are not qualities that warrant a valuable seat on the "good to great" bus you are supposed to be driving as a leader of your organization.

Further, some of these employees who are not getting the job done in terms of output or attitude may have personal situations that make the decisions to let them go more difficult. I'm talking about single moms, sole breadwinners, those caring for a sick child or parent, and so on. In one case, I had a client who had to fire a poorly performing department head who was dealing with stage 3 cancer—no one said being a leader was for the faint of heart. However, as the graphic, real-life examples in this chapter demonstrate, taking a hard look at unproductive or negative team players, coaching and mentoring them to improve and, if they don't, ultimately letting them go, is what all good leaders must do. Anything less shows weakness, promotes mediocrity, and demoralizes and demotivates the best people on your team. Not to mention that it has a seriously negative impact on your organization's productivity, effectiveness, and bottom line.

15

Change Is the Only Constant

Great leadership involves many factors, the biggest being how one deals with change. Change is a funny thing. We all know intellectually that it is inevitable, but we sometimes resist or fight it as if this were a real option. But the great leaders embrace change. They understand that, while it may be scary and unnerving, change also offers opportunities to challenge oneself as well as members of your own team to be more creative, flexible and strategic.

In his classic book, *Who Moved My Cheese?*, Dr. Spencer Johnson tells a simple but powerful story about four characters in a maze who are obsessed with finding cheese. Two of the characters are mice named Sniff and Scurry and two are "little people," Hem and Haw, who are as small as mice but have a very different approach to finding cheese. The cheese is a metaphor for anything we want or desire in life. It could be a great job, a terrific company with flowing profits, or the relationship of your dreams. The maze, says Johnson, is "where you look for what you want—the organization you work in or the family or community you live in."[1] In business and in life, change is the only constant, yet all four characters in the book see it very differently. The mice expect it, revel in it, and actually figure out how to have fun looking for new cheese as the old cheese disappears. However, Hem and Haw seem constantly frustrated, resentful, and angry. But the cheese they were convinced they earned and owned is no longer where they expected. According to Johnson, "It would all be so easy if you had a map to the maze. If the same old routines worked. If they just stopped moving 'the cheese,' but things keep changing."[2]

And so it is today in organizational life. Old paradigms no longer apply. Economics and markets keep changing. We have new competitors every day, and the economy is often so unpredictable that those who buy our goods and services sometimes want more for less. It also seems harder than ever before to bring in those prospective customers sitting on the fence. The leaders of many organizations as well as individuals refuse to see the handwriting on the wall and just hope that things will get better. Yet, wishful thinking is no substitute for a strategic plan. Real leaders recognize that these outside forces and changing landscapes often require changes within their own organization (including change in how a leader thinks). These leaders not only come up with real solutions and partnerships, but they constantly motivate and inspire team members to get past their fear of change and rise to the challenge.

These leaders also communicate that vision for how the team must deal with the change. They speak in a compelling and clear fashion what is needed to survive and grow and who needs to do what on the team. It is not enough to simply have the vision; great leaders must find the words and set an example for others to see and follow.

When Leading Change, Every Detail Matters

Clearly, leading a successful change effort requires several key elements, including a strong leader who engages team members with a sense of urgency, and talks about what exactly needs to be done by when. Successfully leading change also requires that you have the right team who can execute, perform, and get the job done right. Consider the case of President Barack Obama's revolutionary efforts to change the way the American citizens obtain healthcare. As is the case with any change, challenge is to be expected. Of course, people were going to push back, be uncomfortable, or simply be confused. Yet, the people in the Obama administration knew that this would be better in the long run and understood that they would need to push through all of the negativity to see their initiative through to the other side. When you're going through a monster of a change, it is imperative that all i's are dotted and t's are crossed and that you as a leader are doing everything necessary to ensure a smooth transition. While those involved may have had the best intentions, this did not happen.

Which brings us to the fall of 2013, when President Obama finally attempted to address the serious problems connected to the malfunctioning of the Affordable Care Act website. In fact, at that time the site wasn't close to where it was supposed to be. It simply didn't allow those who went online to navigate it and sign up for health insurance. In response, President Obama said they needed to "scrub the site" of "glitches." He also said "nobody is madder than me" and that the website problem is a "good problem to have." When leading change, persuasive speeches are helpful at the beginning to move people, but understanding the importance of executing on the details is even more important because when things consistently break down, people lose confidence that you and your team can get the job done. The problems with HealthCare.gov in the fall of 2013 were not "glitches" and they were surely not "good problems to have." When leading change, every detail matters.

Analyzing Obamacare from a policy or political perspective is not my objective in this chapter; rather, it's understanding some of the key reasons why the much publicized HealthCare.gov website failed to work the way it was supposed to on October 1, 2013. Further, the lessons the rest of us can learn from what happened are very important for leaders embracing change. Consider the following steps when you institute your own changes:

- Instill a sense of urgency. Many in the federal government knew for well over a year that October 1, 2013, was the deadline for the implementation of the healthcare exchange. It appears that, leading up to this date, no responsible government leader was sending the message that there were serious problems and that reinforcements were needed. After the initial failures on October 1, President Obama spoke to the nation in a very calm, relaxed manner, said that consumers had six months to sign up and implied the exchange "glitches" were nothing to worry about. His message changed dramatically in the weeks that followed, and ultimately there was a real sense of urgency—if not panic, to get it right. But by then, it was too late.

• Have the right people on your team. Clearly such a complex initiative such as the healthcare exchange marketplace and website required that the most talented and technologically capable experts were on board from the start. But were they? At the time, when the Secretary of Health and Human Services, Kathleen Sebelius, said after a series of embarrassing website debacles that we "have asked the contractors to bring their A team to the table" one has to wonder why the "A team" wasn't brought in from day one.[3] The irony is that these external folks with strong technical abilities were ultimately brought in to fix or undo what the original team Sebelius had put together screwed up in the first place.

• Make no excuses. While the president eventually stated that there is "no excuse" for technical problems with the website when later speaking about the issues with the HealthCare.gov rollout, this was not his initial response when things first went wrong. In fact, his initial response was filled with excuses, including the erroneous argument that the Internet-based program wasn't working because the demand from consumers going online simply overwhelmed the system. Not true. Rather, the system was inherently flawed. Strong leaders make no excuses right from the start, while weaker leaders change their narrative when backed into a corner because the initial excuses didn't cut it.

• Call a time-out. Great leaders have the courage and practical insight to simply *stop* when enough information indicates that the original plan is seriously flawed. There was enough reason to call a time-out and push the October 1 deadline to a later date well before President Obama did. Would it have been embarrassing? Yes, but not nearly as embarrassing as what, ultimately, happened by waiting. Strong leadership requires that you acknowledge when things are not working as planned and then come up with a plan B.

The Keys to Leading Change

Clearly, leading big change is not for the faint of heart. So what are the keys to leading and embracing change in these very difficult and challenging times? Consider the following list of tips and tools that will be extremely helpful to you and your team when leading change:

- Accentuate the positives, but don't act as if there won't be challenges. People know that's simply not true. Being honest and having a positive "we can do this" attitude about those challenges is a key to leading change, because a leader of change has to be credible. Remember, even if a change is challenging or difficult, many team members will "buy in" if they believe in *you* as a leader, because the messenger is often at least as important as the message about change.

    Simply put, a big part of establishing this credibility and trust is recognizing the obstacles and challenges present, while communicating confidence that they can be overcome. According to John Kotter, an expert on change management who has examined over one hundred companies trying to reengineer themselves, "Sometimes the obstacle is organizational structure. . . . Sometimes compensation or performance appraisal systems make people choose between the new vision and their own self-interest. . . . Worst of all are the bosses who refuse to change and who make demands that are inconsistent with the overall effort."[4]

Whatever the obstacles to change are, they must be addressed and overcome. If there are particular people in the organization who are resisting change, those people must be convinced that it is in their interest to be a part of the transformation. There are many ways to persuade and get "buy-in." The key, however, is to make the effort. To ignore obstacles, or to pretend there will be none, is to invite failure.

- Explain *why* the change is taking place. If people see this as "change for the sake of change," it's going to fail. Further, don't be the leader that tries to direct people to change by telling them "just do it" or "because I said so." The problem here is that many people in the organization won't believe the change is necessary if it is unclear *why* the change must take place. The key is for those leading change to make it clear that the status quo is actually more dangerous and risky than the change itself. Until that's done, people have little or no motivation to buy into the process.

  People are naturally resistant to change, and therefore, for many, changing is unnatural. This fact of life cannot be ignored. The leaders who believe that people should follow them in implementing a particular change, simply because they are "in charge" or "the boss," just don't get it. Really good leaders understand the importance of making it crystal clear that the risks of *not* changing present concrete and serious problems that the effort to change has the potential to remedy.

- Make it clear what the payoff or tangible benefits of implementing this change will be. As I mention in my earlier point, it is important to explain the risks associated with maintaining the status quo, but it is just as important to share what the positives will be. Don't assume your people know this. It is your job to make it real. Too many organizations try to sell the change through detailed standard operating procedure manuals or highly detailed descriptions of the steps needed to implement the change. The problem with this approach is that people aren't convinced that what the change will produce is a good thing.

What is the vision? How does the change connect to the bigger picture of success? The best leaders have a clear vision and not only articulate *why* the change is taking place but explain what's in it for their people and for the organizations. What are the benefits that will result from the change? This approach is about motivation and persuasion and not about compliance, command, and control. Simply put, it's about real leadership.

- Be clear about the reasons for the change while remaining flexible and open to feedback regarding different approaches to implementing the change. There is nothing worse than leaders who are rigid and closed-minded about anything other than their own ideas.
- Create an open environment conducive to an honest dialogue, even if the feedback is difficult to hear. This approach allows team members to comment on any aspect of the change without fear of reprisal or retribution. Do this because team members are thinking these things anyway. Open dialogue can be created in forums, employee meetings, interactive e-mail, or a one-on-one with the team leader. Further, the truly great change leaders anticipate pushback and are prepared to facilitate a candid conversation around it. These leaders have the courage and confidence to proactively bring up potential opposition before anyone else because they're not afraid of it. They confront it. They deal with it directly and take it on by making the case that the status quo is absolutely not acceptable.
- Celebrate and recognize any success or accomplishment associated with the change effort, no matter how small. People need to see progress in order to buy into the change. Everyone wants to be part of a winning team.
- Finally, never forget as a leader that real change about real problems and issues is a marathon, not a sprint. Organizational leaders often don't understand how hard leading change can be and therefore become highly impatient with how slow the process is. Leaders will often become frustrated with their people and let them know it—a reaction that only makes the

change harder to implement. Think about it: How leaders see change is one thing. They are the ones often driving the process. However, employees see it differently. They are the ones that change is happening to. Successful change agents understand that they must empathize and understand the position of their employees and act accordingly.

Further, change takes time, and leaders looking for a "quick fix" or some kind of "immediate turnaround" will be deeply disappointed. There are no magic or silver bullets in the change business. And there are definitely none in leadership. There are only hard work, dedication, and persistence to pursue constant improvement that seeks organizational excellence. Additionally, beware of what I call "change fatigue," which occurs when you propose too many changes over too short a period of time. You will wear your people out.

Obviously, change isn't easy. We all seek stability and predictability. But today more than ever, change keeps hitting us in the face just when we think we can afford to get comfortable. So stop fighting change. It is of no use, and complaining about change isn't a viable option, particularly for those of us in positions of leadership, because the last time I checked, "change is the only constant."

16

Big Shoes to Fill

Effective Succession Planning

Succession planning. It's easy to talk a good game when it comes to planning for who will lead the future of an organization, but actually doing it is a different story. Every organization—whether it's a large corporation, a family-run business, or a small mom-and-pop shop—must have a strong plan of succession and a few leaders ready to step up and take charge when the current boss steps aside or is forced out for health or other reasons. Yet, we find more and more that even in the most sophisticated and visible companies, no realistic and practical succession plan exists. Why is this? And how much of this leadership failure is a product of the way the leader of an organization handles this highly personal issue? Clearly, succession planning is a rational and logical strategy that must be done well.

There are many reasons for leaders to think seriously about and plan for their succession; however, we must ask why succession planning is so difficult for so many.

First, particularly in cases where the leader created the organization, leaders often have a tremendous personal and emotional investment and don't want to move aside. They don't even want to think about the possibility. The same passion and commitment that allowed such leaders to work tirelessly to build the organization causes them to resist giving up control.

For many of the clients to whom I provide leadership development coaching, I have found that succession planning has been particularly challenging for the CEOs, especially when an organization's success and brand is so closely tied to its leader. Yes, it's the "cult of personality" phenomenon. Consider the case of Lee Iacocca. Back in the 1970s, given the endless string of highly successful TV commercials, it was impossible to imagine Chrysler without its CEO, Lee Iacocca. This is not necessarily a bad thing. In fact, this type of leader often conveys a sense of passion, a commitment to excellence, and a level of loyalty that many others lack or are incapable of producing, because of a variety of factors. Yet, the downside comes when this charismatic and highly visible leader remains as the CEO for a decade, or even two or more, or he or she is over seventy yet continues to perform well. It's all good, right? Well, you see, there's one catch—this leader can't live forever. Even if he or she is the most vibrant and healthy leader around, living forever just isn't an option, the last time I checked. So having a successful succession plan is an absolute must if the organization is to continue to thrive.

One of the biggest obstacles or challenges many companies face is an organizational mindset that you can actually find another Lee or another "Joe," the fictitious name we'll give to the hugely successful, highly unique, and charismatic leader of your organization. Well, you're *not* going to find another Joe. There isn't another Joe, so stop looking for one. This approach winds up being just one more reason why Joe himself, and those around him, fail to put together a realistic succession plan.

Once those leading the succession planning process have accepted this fact, they must stop themselves from thinking it's impossible to find a successor for Joe at all. It's not. It may be challenging, but it can also be a terrific opportunity to identify a new leader, with a different way of doing things, who can infuse new energy and a fresh vision for the organization. Yet, this will only happen if Joe as a leader and those around him choose to seize this opportunity.

When an organization is planning to replace a legendary, or even merely successful, CEO, it is immensely important to avoid framing the process by looking in the rearview mirror. This is because what a company needs in the next six months and beyond may be drastically different from what was needed even over the past few months. In fact, an individual who sees the company and its industry through a new set of eyes may be the person best prepared to recognize and seize new opportunities for the organization. Do not be afraid to select a successor who is quite unlike his or her predecessor. What worked in the past will not necessarily work in the future. It is more important that the organization defines the skill set, expertise, and character required for the next CEO by taking into consideration the company's future needs. With this framework in mind, the smart leader commits to finding the future leader that fits this mold. We all know that our business environment is dynamic and ever-changing. Why then would we not be vigilant in looking forward when selecting the leader who will carry our organization in that direction?

Another reason succession planning is so challenging for some leaders is that potential future leaders, who are talented enough to actually step up and take over, often get pushed out because their presence makes CEOs uncomfortable. This is where things get highly personal, and potentially complicated. In fact, this is where emotional intelligence really kicks in. If "Joe" can only see himself as a complete person if he is serving as a leader of this particular organization, then how realistic is it to expect that he would help identify his replacement? It's not. Of course, we want leaders who are committed to organizational success and who are "all in" with passion and enthusiasm and are willing to do what it takes to succeed. However, truly well-rounded leaders also have other interests and passions beyond their work—family, hobbies, friends, relationships, and so on. The problem is that if Joe's total existence is based on his role as the leader in this particular position, he will likely have an unhealthy view about moving forward. He will be hesitant to help develop those around him and plan for the organization's future without him, which is in fact one of a leader's most important roles.

We all have insecurities. I know I have mine. We want to see ourselves as irreplaceable. Often, we want to imagine that we are better than everyone else, not only in our organization but, possibly, in our industry. The leadership lesson is that truly successful leaders understand the psychological and emotional dynamics at play here and put things in the proper perspective. Such leaders understand that a big part of their legacy is, in fact, the ability to actually help identify and, yes, develop future leaders of the organization—including their potential successor. Doing this is anything but a knock or slight against the leaders' ability because others are capable of moving the ship forward. Rather, if done successfully, being a major part of the succession planning effort for leaders should be a huge feather in their caps.

Also, boards of directors may be reluctant to confront the succession-planning issue head-on. Board members can sometimes be too close to the current CEO and not want to go through the candid and uncomfortable "What happens if . . ." conversation that must take place, so they ignore, they punt, they placate—and when the need arises for a new leader to step in, it is often too late. That's why one of the most important leadership lessons when it comes to putting a board of trustees or directors together is to not simply pick your closest friends. Leaders must have the courage and foresight to seek out and recruit board members who are leaders in their respective fields, who have expertise and traits that they themselves lack. Further, leaders should recruit board members who can be trusted to consistently and strategically challenge them when there is legitimate disagreement and not simply go along because they are intimidated or because their close friendship precludes them from doing so.

Another leadership lesson regarding succession can be learned from the leaders who, contrary to those who may resist or fight the process, instead try to micromanage and control it. I'm talking about the ones who cut others out and take the "I've got this" approach to what should instead be a process that gains the input and feedback from a variety of key stakeholders. In consulting for one major Fortune 500 organization, I asked the company's CEO if there was a legitimate succession plan in place. He replied, "Absolutely. Bob is my succession plan. He has been with me for years and knows this place like the back of his hand. He'll be the guy to take over when I go." This approach may be fine for a mom-and-pop shop, but for any organization that is complex, multilayered, and has a number of employees and stakeholders, it is not only simplistic, but dangerous.

A successful succession plan cannot be created in a vacuum. It can't be hatched in the mind of the CEO without active participation from an independent and concerned board. An open, candid, and yes, difficult series of conversations must take place with all major parties involved. The pros and cons of potential leaders must be put on the table. Even if the current CEO is convinced that "Bob is the guy," what happens if Bob is not the choice of the majority of the board or if Bob doesn't have the confidence of the staff? What happens if key stakeholders and industry leaders think Bob is a puppet for the current CEO and doesn't have what it takes to lead? These are just some of the questions that make succession planning so difficult but essential. Further, this is why leaders should never be allowed or be in a position to control every aspect of their own succession.

With this in mind, consider the following leadership lessons when it comes to succession planning:

- Remember that CEO succession planning is *not* a single-person event. When organizations take on succession planning, they often focus on the CEO role and neglect to focus on other positions as well. However, the best succession planning involves a constant assembly and reassembly of a leadership puzzle with many pieces. As each piece of the leadership puzzle is put in place—be it the CEO, CFO, COO, or other positions—the shape of the remaining pieces will become clearer. Simply put, the choice of the best candidate to succeed the current CEO will depend in part on the team of people surrounding the new leader and how all of their individual skill sets complement one another.

The leadership lesson here is to never consider solely who will replace the CEO, but rather see succession planning as an organization-wide initiative. The really smart leaders tie succession planning to larger leadership development efforts. In fact, one of my clients, who had been thinking a lot about (and, possibly, struggling with) his own succession wound up feeling a lot more comfortable about the overall succession-planning process upon realizing that multiple department heads and senior leaders within the organization were approaching retirement age. Thus, he recognized that it was critical to identify not only who would succeed him but who the future leaders of the organization working alongside his successor would be. Together we developed a Leadership Academy in which these potential future leaders received extensive executive one-on-one coaching. These individuals were also placed into small group sessions I facilitated in which they collaborated and shared ideas about the leadership challenges they face every day. By doing this, not only did the future leaders develop important leadership skills and tools but, in the process, the organization came to realize that some of these individuals were not as strong as originally thought. Therefore, their place in the succession plan was changed dramatically. The point here is that succession planning should not be solely about one person who will lead the organization, but rather it should be about how the organization develops its bench of talent and mentors future leaders to take on important roles within the organization moving forward. This can only happen if the organization's leaders are committed to such an effort and create such a culture. Further, taking this approach will make the CEO's succession a more natural and organic part of the process.

- Even when great internal candidates exist, continue to look outside for other prospective candidates. Doing otherwise is simply not a smart strategy. Having a viable internal candidate should never stop the succession-planning team from considering outside candidates. Simply put, an effective succession-planning process must include internal and external candidates to ensure that all of the best candidates for the job are considered. Once the succession-planning team has identified the key candidates outside of the organization, the next step is to then compare these candidates with the best players internally. Be sure to evaluate these candidates using the same focus on forward-looking skills and experience criteria I discussed earlier in this chapter.

- Don't be convinced that the candidate has to be "ready now." As I've said—and discuss in great detail in chapter 9—great leaders are great coaches and mentors, and they are aware that a critical part of succession planning is to prepare their successor for his or her new role. Truly exceptional leaders invest the time and effort necessary to develop the organization's leaders of the future. For example, when considering candidates internally, you must first identify the handful of "A" players on your team that show the capacity to get results as well as build the relationships necessary to make these results sustainable over time. Next, include these high-potential leaders in conversations and meetings that will expose them to people and challenges that they would not have experience with on their own. Further, stretch your succession candidates by giving them challenging project assignments or jobs that round out their foundation of experience. If they've historically focused on internal activities, give them the opportunity to work with external partners or to try their hand at a client-facing role. If they've been more focused on the external aspects of the business, give them assignments that will put them in a position to interact with many different colleagues and build the operational muscles necessary to run critical activities internally.

An important leadership lesson, which I advocate for any leader mentoring any team members, is to never stop coaching these succession candidates in their development. Ask questions that help them review what they have learned from each experience and stretch assignment, and help them apply this learning to what may be coming up in their future. If you don't have the time or the inclination to coach them yourself, consider eliciting the help of an external expert or developing a Leadership Academy as previously mentioned. Whatever you do, don't simply throw your successor into the deep end without any support. As the outgoing leader, you do not want to leave them in a position to simply "sink or swim."

- Don't keep succession plans a secret. Be up front. Really confident and secure leaders should have the ability and willingness to talk openly about their succession. It shouldn't be embarrassing. In fact, when you decide that you will be stepping aside, you should say so. Again, you must make it clear how the process will work and who will be involved in the succession planning effort. Conversely, if you don't do this, then ask yourself, who and what will fill up the vacuum when it comes to information? How about the rumor mill? We love rumors. We love gossip. It's human nature. So remember, if you're thinking about stepping aside but have convinced yourself that not talking about it or keeping it a secret is a smart strategy—it's not. This is especially true for organizations that have recently experienced a lot of change. In these cases, people are particularly inclined to be uneasy and insecure about their future. As a leader, be up front and share plans. Efforts to foster transparency will go a long way in combating any perception of a hidden agenda and will in turn reassure your people that you are considering their needs as well as the needs of the overall organization. As I said earlier, make succession planning part of a larger organizational roadmap and leadership development game plan and let your people know it.

How Far Does the Apple Fall from the Tree?

Let's talk about family-owned or -operated organizations and succession planning. This is something I know a lot about, since my father founded and was the leader for over forty years of a major not-for-profit organization that runs a first-rate charter school operation, a pre-K, and daycare program serving hundreds of children, has built housing, and is involved in economic development and a variety of training and social service programs, as well as serving senior citizens. As hard as succession planning is in the corporate world with no blood relations, it becomes even more challenging when siblings and old family rivalries come into play. Instead of simply thinking about what's best for the organization, certain family members may have a hard time separating their strong dislike or distrust for a relative from the organization's needs. When family is involved, jealousy, history and pettiness become heightened. Family-run businesses can be great because everyone has a tremendous stake in the organization's success, but when the time comes to plan for the succession of the matriarch or patriarch, often all hell breaks loose.

In fact, I argue that one of the most important leadership lessons in the case of family businesses is to realize that the organization's successor does not have to come from within the family. Yet, leaders often have children and siblings, many of whom see themselves as the rightful successor. Frankly, in choosing the best leader, these family relationships are only one of many factors to consider. While they are part of the dynamics of the organization, smart leaders know these relationships cannot be the only influencing factor in choosing their successor—it's just unrealistic. So the best-case scenario is for such an organization to have a different approach to succession planning that's not strictly based on bloodline. This can only happen if the leader has the wisdom and the courage to execute this plan, and I have seen few who fall into this category. In fact, according to PwC's Family Business Survey of 2013, 76 percent of U.S. family business leaders surveyed believed the best way to fulfill the founder's dreams was to keep the business in the family. Yet, only half of these leaders expected that members of the next generation could do it on their own. Among those who were not confident in the abilities of their bloodline, uncertainty about junior members' aptitude for running a company was cited as their leading concern.[1]

Understanding this reality, strong leaders of family-owned or -operated organizations should establish a highly independent board or separate committee, whose sole responsibility is to identify a potential group of successors and to ultimately help choose the best candidate. Further, the leader of such an organization should also realize that there is a distinct possibility that the organization will decide it needs a leader with the kind of skills and tools that simply do not exist within the family. The succession planning, therefore, should also consider candidates outside of the family. In the vast majority of family-run businesses, this suggestion would likely be rejected outright by one or more family members. So if this is the case and the leader feels it necessary to take a strong hand in selecting the organization's next leader from within the family ranks, I say there is one critical next step. This leader must identify the leadership traits that are absolutely essential and then conduct a thorough and objective review of the potential candidates within the family.

Ultimately, if the leader insists on making the final choice—the choice must be based on merit. One of the biggest leadership lessons when it comes to succession planning is to not simply pick your son or daughter because of their bloodlines. Very often, such a decision could be disastrous for everyone else involved. A truly great leader needs to have the character and courage to stand up to whatever criticism or likely resistance exists by picking the best candidate from within the family ranks, even if it is a distant cousin, because that person possesses the required leadership traits and has been selected based on merit. Succession planning is a complex and complicated process, and it takes a special kind of leader to play an integral and valuable role in his or her succession. Yet, it is doable and the payoff is lasting and significant on many levels.

17

Leading Successful Integration

Maintaining the status quo is very rarely an option for leaders these days. Mergers, acquisitions, and strategic alliances—they are all more common than ever. Full disclosure: I am currently coaching or consulting for several organizations that have either recently gone through some type of merger or will soon be merging, acquiring, or entering into a strategic alliance—which I have found typically evolves into a deeper and more complex relationship. In fact, I'm working with one CEO who is proactively leading the effort to find the appropriate suitor to merge his organization with because he is convinced that after years of going it alone, such a bold move will give his organization its best chance of succeeding in the highly competitive and rapidly changing marketplace. During one of our meetings, I had a fascinating conversation with this CEO when I bluntly said, "Bob, you do know that if you succeed in this effort, there's a very good chance that you're going to put yourself out of a job?"

My question was referring to the fact that he was seeking to merge with a larger organization that would probably have the organizational and financial leverage to name its own CEO, who would likely replace him, and further, there was no guarantee that he would find a place on the executive team. Bob's response to me was revealing and also offered a powerful lesson for all leaders. He said, "Steve, I just turned sixty. I've put in over thirty years in this business. I would love to spend another five to ten years doing this job, but there's no way we can continue on our current track and have the organization succeed. The only chance we have is to create the right strategic relationship and merge with a partner who will help us achieve what we need to achieve as an organization. If that means that I'm merged out of a job, then that's the way it's going to be. I have to do the right thing, not for myself, but for the thousands of people that I am responsible for as employees. Not to mention all of the people we serve every day as clients."

Do you want an example of great leadership that you'll never see in a *Wall Street Journal* or *New York Times* headline? There it is. A leader who understands that sometimes strategically merging or being acquired, and putting aside his ego in the process, is the right thing to do for the larger good of his company. The most effective leaders understand that there are times when merging, acquiring, or creating substantial strategic alliances is the only way to thrive, much less survive, in these very difficult times. The really great leaders don't just have the intellect to do this; they also have the maturity to rationally and dispassionately evaluate all options and then do what's best for the organization.

Yet, leaders involved in mergers, acquisitions, and other related organizational restructuring activities know that this is no easy feat. Further, no matter how you go about this process, you *will* make enemies. Some people will hold on dearly to the status quo, believing there's no need to make such drastic moves. Some, even those who accept there is a need to merge or be acquired, will criticize or question your negotiation skills. Some will say you gave up too much, while others will complain that you didn't give in enough and that you're too stubborn. Yet, everyone who has an opinion about how a leader handles a merger, acquisition, or a strategic alliance has an agenda, and that agenda is usually narrow and parochial. It's based on self-preservation and survival. Now, this doesn't make these people bad or evil—it makes them human. All we have to do is reference Abraham Maslow's hierarchy of needs, in which preserving ourselves remains our most basic human instinct.

While many in the organization may be focused on self-preservation, truly great leaders must understand the lesson that they don't always have that option. These leaders can't afford to be parochial or myopic. Yet, leaders who have the vision, emotional intelligence, and courage to see the forest from the trees and who ultimately act on what is best for the larger organization are very unique indeed. Even with all of the right tips and tools and with the right attitude, I've seen numerous leaders make egregious mistakes in handling mergers and acquisitions on both ends of the deal. I've seen leaders who were part of the larger organization that was acquiring or merging with a smaller one make a challenging situation a lot worse. But I've also seen the opposite in cases where the organization that was being taken over was led by people who just made things worse, because they lacked a true understanding of not only what their people were feeling but also how to help those same people see the process as an opportunity as opposed to a death sentence.

Don't get me wrong; none of this is easy and much of it can be scary. Often, people *will* lose their jobs in a merger or an acquisition. Simply put, you don't need two CEOs or two directors of finance. However, it's not so black-and-white, and the really smart leaders understand that. I've worked with too many people who have acted as if the merger itself somehow guaranteed a particular outcome— either a positive one or a terrible one—a mindset that ultimately contributed to a self-fulfilling prophecy. Translation: it's not the merger or the acquisition itself that guarantees a particular outcome. Rather, it is the conduct of a leader or manager over the course of the process that can give other key decision makers a particular impression of that person and influence his or her future accordingly.

I've also worked with leaders who say all the right things about the need to "integrate" two organizations into one but who are not truly honest about the significant cultural differences between the two entities. In one case, years after a particular merger, the integration effort continued to struggle because organizational leaders never set up a mechanism for employees from both organizations to talk openly about their concerns, fears, hopes, and goals. As I discuss in detail in chapter 15, which explores how to lead and embrace change, by not establishing such a feedback channel, the leader creates a vacuum that becomes consumed with rumors and all sorts of half-truths just because people don't know what's happening and start guessing. It's human nature. I have also seen integration efforts with mergers and acquisitions in which leaders insist on communicating with an iron fist. Often, in these cases, leaders delude themselves into thinking that they can shut things down and stop the rumor mill by not holding any town hall meetings or forums and, instead, insisting that the legal department has demanded that there be no open dialogue about what's happening. That leadership approach is dangerous indeed. Of course, there *are* legal restrictions when organizations are merging with or acquiring one another. But that doesn't mean that *nothing* can be said and that no information can be shared. When leaders go "radio silent" and hide behind the legal department as an excuse for saying nothing, once again, it only creates more fear and anxiety.

Don't get me wrong—I'm not saying leaders should share information haphazardly just to demonstrate that they are open and honest with their organization. In fact, talking hypothetically about what could happen in a merger is just as dangerous, if not more dangerous, for leaders than saying nothing at all. When I coached one CEO for a major employee forum he was about to hold, I advised that under no circumstances should he answer hypothetical questions. There were simply too many variables and factors for him to take into account, which made it too risky to attempt to respond in a clear fashion. Sure enough, the third question the CEO was asked by a very nervous employee was "Given the merger that's about to happen, how many employees could potentially be let go?" This was exactly the kind of hypothetical question smart leaders know not to answer in a public forum. It wasn't a question of being candid or up front, it's a question that shouldn't be answered because the answer was unknown. At the time, there were too many variables and undecided questions and issues to be resolved to have a clear sense of such a number. So how did the leader in this situation respond?

At first, the CEO explained that he couldn't really predict such a number. Yet, in a matter of seconds another employee pressed the issue, saying, "Could it be as many as 5,000 employees?" In this moment, the leader cracked and said, "That's possible but it's no guarantee." There it is. What do you think most people walked out of that public forum thinking? You got it—that 5,000 people were about to be laid off because of a merger that was about to happen. So what did some of the best people in the organization start doing? Well, what would *you* do if you were one of those people? You'd update your résumé and start looking for another job. That's exactly what happened.

The problem with the statement this leader made, in such a critical and open setting, isn't only that the answer was incorrect; it was irresponsible for him to say such a thing in public. The lesson he just didn't understand was that responding to hypothetical questions about the potential impact of a merger, especially regarding possible layoffs, has no upside. It would have been different if he had known for sure exactly how many employees were going to be let go; however, that is rarely the case. When I pressed the CEO as to why he said what he did, his response was that he felt backed into a corner. He clearly wasn't. Rather, he was inexperienced and panicked. Instead, he should have stuck to his initial response: that there were too many variables and unknowns to predict such a number at that point in time.

With this scenario in mind, and realizing that most leaders will eventually face the need to integrate in connection with a merger, an acquisition, or a strategic organizational alliance of some form, consider the following leadership lessons:

- Don't be afraid to say, "I don't know." If you're not sure or you just simply don't know at a particular point in time, then say so. Sometimes leaders confuse being candid with making up a specific response when they don't even have one. The irony is that candor and honesty sometimes calls for the leader to say,

"At this point, we haven't resolved that issue, but as soon as we do, we will hold a public forum, announce it, and have an open discussion with all of you." That's telling the truth, and more leaders need to be comfortable simply saying, "I don't know."

- Assign one of your top people to handle the day-to-day integration effort. I'm talking the nuts and bolts, the nitty-gritty. As the leader of the overall organization, you can provide the vision, but it is optimal to have someone in the trenches running those meetings and dealing with the conflicts, personalities, and operational details. An important leadership lesson for CEOs and for any leader driving an integration effort is to never assume that you will be able to handle the day-to-day minutia and still keep your eye on the big picture. Rather, pick one of your best operational "get it done" people for that role, with a direct line to you, and ensure he or she gives you regular updates on where things stand.

- Draft players based on skill set and merit when building your new team. One of the biggest mistakes made when organizations merge is deciding to put people in key leadership positions based too much on politics and "horse trading," as opposed to who is in fact the best person to be in the position. I saw this recently when two large organizations came together and the larger one got to pick the CEO of the newly formed company. As a form of compromise, the COO came from the smaller entity; however, there were real questions about the person picked for this role and whether she was the most qualified. The problem with this approach is that these leaders—who are put in positions to appease or mollify—are often miscast and do not perform particularly well. Ultimately, it is not uncommon for this person to be replaced within a short period of time. A valuable leadership lesson is to look at your talent pool in both organizations from the very beginning of the integration process and put the best people in the right seats on the bus based purely on qualifications and skill set. The more a leader does this in an integration effort, the more successful this effort will be.

- Acknowledge that two very different organizational cultures are being asked to come together, which is in many ways unnatural. It's like two families being asked to live under one roof and not only peacefully coexist but live under one set of norms and values. Could your family do that easily? I know my family would have a very tough time. But that's exactly what a merger or an acquisition and, ultimately, a successful integration is all about. The really smart leaders decide to establish one "new culture" that takes the best of what each team brings to the table and starts to live that culture from day one—not just in words, but also in deeds. The leader's actions must reflect this new culture in meetings, in decisions, in the way the organization is branded internally and externally, as well as in the way people are promoted and rewarded but also escorted off the proverbial bus for poor performance. The sooner the leader acknowledges that two cultures cannot exist under one roof successfully and that a new culture must be established, the greater the potential for the integration effort to succeed.
- Hold very open and public forums in which employees have the opportunity to ask any question on any topic related to the merger, acquisition, or integration. As I mentioned earlier, this helps cut down on the spread of gossip and misinformation. Further, the more you make it clear that you are confident and can handle anything that comes up, the more the people within the organization will sense that there is nothing to hide. Again, this doesn't mean that every employee will survive. (In most cases, one of the reasons for a merger or acquisition is to create economies of scale, which means that some duplicative functions need to be eliminated.) However, the more you are seen as up front and out front, talking openly, honestly, and with confidence about these changes—even when you don't have all of the answers—the greater the chance there will be to build the kind of trust necessary to move forward in the challenging times that clearly lie ahead.

18

Think You Know It All? Think Again

One of the characteristics of a great leader is making a commitment to being a lifelong learner. Change is a constant. It is all around us. We have no choice. But growth is a conscious decision. The greatest leaders make a decision that they want to grow and learn. They want to know more and understand different ways to be more effective at their craft.

The great Spanish cellist and composer Pablo Casals was once asked at age ninety-five why he continued to practice six hours a day. Casals responded, "Because I think I am making progress." Exceptional professionals like Pablo Casals make a commitment to being the best in their respective fields. That's what great leaders do. They read, they research, they ask questions of colleagues, they are curious, they take seminars, they go online, and they are responsive to executive coaching and seek constant advice and feedback.

But what strikes me, after years of conducting leadership development work, is how many professionals have come to the conclusion that where they are today is where they are going to be for the rest of their careers. My colleague at Seton Hall University,

Mike Reuter, who writes a blog on leadership that he posts every Sunday, disagrees. His blog is inspiring and has been really helpful for me. For example, on September 21, 2014, Reuter published a column titled "Fill Your Life with Firsts," in which he points out a powerful message about leaders and lifelong learning. He concludes with a quote from Bill Taylor, co-founder and editor of *Fast Company* magazine: "The challenge for leaders is not to out-hustle, out-muscle, or out-maneuver the competition. It is to out-think the competition in ways big and small, to develop a unique point of view about the future and get there before anyone else does. The best leaders I've gotten to know aren't just the boldest thinkers; they are the most insatiable learners."[1]

With these inspirational and prophetic words in mind, consider a conversation I had several months ago with a top-level insurance executive who was serving as the COO of her company. "Jane" was discussing the importance of developing younger talent in the organization and said, "These kids need stronger executive presence. They need to be better presenters at meetings, and they also need basic management skills."

However, when I asked Jane what kind of help could be provided to more senior executives in the firm, like herself, without hesitation she responded by saying, "Come on, Steve. Don't be ridiculous. I'm in my late forties. How much could anyone teach me at this point? I am pretty much who I am and who I am going to be. The way I communicate today is the way I've communicated for the past twenty years. What you see is what you get."

So there it is. Think about the implications of such a statement and also consider that Jane is representative of countless other professionals in high-level positions who are convinced that either they can't or they won't change or even slightly tweak their leadership approach. What these people are saying is that if they are not listening the way they should be, that is just the way it is. If their presentations are long and rambling and they lose the attention of their audience, well, their audience is just going to have to live with it. If their e-mails are unnecessarily confrontational and negative, that is just who they are. If the meetings they lead are terrible, so be it. That makes no sense. These people are simply giving up.

What is of greater concern for organizations being led by such individuals is that these leadership deficiencies have a significant impact on organizational productivity as well as on those with whom they work—projects aren't getting done, opportunities are missed, and fellow employees are being turned off. Further, the message they are sending to younger, less experienced employees is that making a commitment to professional self-development throughout one's career just isn't important.

It sounds so benign to say, "I am pretty much who I am and who I am going to be," but the implications of such a simplistic statement for leaders in important positions must be considered. It's one thing when leaders think they are stuck at a certain level and can't learn any more. But what about those who are convinced they know it all? Just last month, as I was working on this book and leading a seminar at a major insurance company on the West Coast, a top executive in the group whom I will call "Jim Smith," made it clear that he felt there was nothing he could learn from our work together. The twenty-five industry leaders in the seminar, colleagues of Jim, were responding to one of my initial seminar questions, in which I ask the participants to identify and discuss their most significant leadership challenge and how they have dealt with it. As the seminar participants shared their leadership experiences, Jim was the only one not engaged. In fact, he turned his back on the entire group and focused on using his phone instead. It was clear to me what he was doing, and so I asked him directly about his most significant leadership challenge. In response, he mumbled something inaudible. It was clear that Jim had no intention of participating.

Later, he would tell others that listening to colleagues describe their greatest leadership challenge and how they tried to resolve the situation had little or no value for him. He would later explain that he "knew all of this" from his "past experience" and that the exercise—in fact, the entire leadership seminar series, which he was mandated to attend—was pointless because "he wasn't going to learn anything new about leadership anyway."

The real irony in this situation is that in my one-on-one executive coaching sessions with Jim, we reviewed the feedback he received from his colleagues through his 360 Leadership Assessment, much of which was that he often came across in meetings "as a know-it-all" and that he "needed to work on being more open to others' points of view."

Think about that. The exact leadership trait or lesson that many of the people who knew Jim Smith best were telling him that he needed to improve upon was the very thing that he felt was a waste of his time because he knew it all already.

It's interesting to note that Jim is very well read and knowledgeable about many topics. In fact, when I first met with him, he proceeded to tell me that he was a "historian and a scholar," that he felt he could easily be the CEO of the company, and that he was "underappreciated by others." He also told me that he had little patience for others' "ignorance." Yet, what Jim clearly doesn't understand and could learn a lot about is the impact that his "I'm the smartest guy in the room" vibe has on those around him. It is a huge turn-off. He makes it clear that he feels has nothing to learn from his peers and sends a powerful and toxic message to people who matter in his professional life about how he views them and their worth—or lack thereof. So consider this, if Jim is sending such a negative message, why should these other leaders go out of their way to help him, support him, or give him the benefit of the doubt in a difficult situation or in negotiation?

Jim Smith has a lot of lessons to learn, not only about leadership, but about the nature of people and what motivates them, as well as what a terrible perception those same people have of him. Further, Jim needs to learn a lot more about himself and why he has this unhealthy and clearly incorrect view that he pretty much knows all about practically everything.

Finally, in the case of both Jane the COO and Jim Smith, we are taught the valuable lesson that as leaders it is dangerous and counterproductive to conclude there is nothing new we can or should learn. For the truly exceptional and ever-improving leaders are, in fact, lifelong learners.

The Keys to Being a Lifelong Learner

Now consider some practical tips that will help you as a leader who wants to learn something new and get better every day:

- Never stop reading. I'm talking about online and journal articles discussing leadership challenges and important topics connected to leadership, such as how to improve the way you lead your meetings, how to deal with difficult conversations, or how to negotiate with an especially challenging adversary. I've also found that reading the work of others in the field of leadership, who have a different perspective from my own, can be especially helpful. One of those authors is Adam Bryant, who writes "The Corner Office," a column in the Business Section of the Sunday *New York Times*. Bryant interviews different leaders every week about how they do what they do and why they have taken their particular approach to leadership. I learn something every time I read one of Bryant's columns or a chapter from his book, *Quick and Nimble*, which Bryant and I have discussed on my public television series, *One-on-One*. In fact, after reading his column for years, I had our public television producers book him for the show. I wanted to learn more, and I felt our viewers could learn more from him as well. The point here is to create a physical as well as virtual "leadership library" in which you have resource material that you can constantly refer to when looking for a different perspective on dealing with challenging leadership situations. The leader who stops reading and learning is dangerously out of touch.
- Seek leadership development, training, and executive coaching. Consider the golfer who wants to improve but refuses to take any advice from a professional coach who knows things about golf that the struggling golfer never even knew existed.

Trust me, I know—I'm that guy. I've been between a 12 and a 14 handicap and have played golf for twenty years. I keep saying I want to improve significantly and get to a 10 or below; yet, every time I work with a golf instructor, I don't keep the commitment. I go back to my old ways. What right do I really have to think I will get that much better? Is it that much different for a leader who is doing the same things, the same way, again and again, but expects a dramatically better outcome? I don't think so. So admit it—you don't have all of the answers as a leader, and you haven't explored all the options or approaches. Then sign up for a seminar, or interview a few executive coaches until you find one you connect with. You have nothing to lose and everything to gain.

• Take each failure or loss that you experience as a leader and decide to see it as an opportunity to learn instead of simply being disappointed or upset. Of course you're not happy about it. I'm never happy when things don't work out professionally as I had planned. However, the really great leaders ask, "What exactly went wrong?" and "What could I or should I, as a leader, have done that would have created a different outcome?" (Sometimes the answer is nothing, because the outcome was beyond your control.) Finally, "What can I learn as a leader, and what can we learn as a team, from this experience that will change the way we deal with similar situations in the future?" Taking this learning attitude and approach in every professional situation, especially the ones that don't turn out as planned, can only improve your leadership and create better results for your team.

It is important to note that this learning tip can only work if you're willing and/or able to accept responsibility for the organization's failure or loss. As you can see from several chapters in this book, one of my biggest and most important leadership lessons involves the need for leaders to be accountable and responsible for the outcome of everything that happens within their organization. The leaders who cannot or will not learn this lesson will be unable to learn from failures or losses, because they will be too busy defending themselves and trying to pin things on someone else.

As leaders, we are constantly getting up at bat, constantly putting ourselves and our organizations out there to be accepted or rejected in the marketplace. Because of this fact, losses are absolutely inevitable. I don't care how good you think you are—they are going to happen. It's the law of averages. So, you might as well be one of those leaders who take a genuine "learning" attitude when these situations inevitably arise.

- Seek out mentors. It would be great if leaders with more experience just organically or naturally found you and offered their help. But it doesn't always work that way. Sometimes you have to proactively identify certain people who you believe have insight and perspectives that would be beneficial to you as a leader. More importantly, the potential mentor must care enough about you and your career to invest the time and effort in helping you grow. I've been fortunate to have had several mentors in my career as a leader. One of the most significant for me has been Ray Bramucci, the late chairman of the board of the nonprofit television production company I've led for a little over twenty years. Ray passed away while I was finishing this book. I had the honor of giving the eulogy at his funeral, which was attended by hundreds of people whom Ray had impacted over the years, and many of whom he had mentored and coached as leaders in various walks of life. Ray had held several senior and executive posts in government as well as in the private sector. He had been chief of staff to former U.S. Senator Bill Bradley and had served as an under secretary in the U.S. Department of Labor in the 1990s. Even as Ray was struggling with serious health issues, every time we spoke he offered wisdom, insight, and perspective on leadership as well as on life that I always found invaluable. Because of Ray's mentoring and friendship over so many years, I know I became a better leader. Without him, and others who have also taken the time and effort to guide me in difficult and challenging times, I would have made many more mistakes about really important matters than the mistakes I've made and fully own. For that I will always be indebted to Ray Bramucci as well as my other mentors over these many years. The message here for all of you leaders reading this book is that having mentors is a must. It's not an option. We all need a few. So the leadership lesson is to pick them wisely and, when you find the right ones, take their advice and never take them for granted.

- Host forums and invite experts into your organization who have a different perspective on important industry issues and topics. Don't just set them up for your team—attend them. You and your people will learn by doing this, and it will also send a powerful message to your team members that you believe learning is essential, not just for them but for you as well, even though you hold a higher position in the organization. Make sure these forums are open and allow for a genuinely candid discussion, which I argue should be facilitated by a professional who knows what he or she is doing. Don't do it yourself. As the leader of the organization, a leadership lesson to consider is that when you play the facilitator role, you run the risk of stifling the conversation and muting honest discourse simply because of the power and influence of your leadership position.

- Ask other leaders about their most significant leadership lesson as well as the most difficult challenge they have faced. I've been doing this over the past year and have gotten responses from over two hundred leaders. I have learned so much just by asking these two questions, as I explain in chapter 1 . None of these leaders were prepped beforehand or told that these questions were coming. Yet, virtually all of them responded in a meaningful way. As a leader, you don't have to be writing a book about leadership or be an anchor on public television to do this. You can do it on your own. Ask a select group of smart leaders whom you know and trust, and you will be surprised at the candor and insight that you get back. I guarantee you will receive important leadership lessons in the process.

These are just some of the ways that leaders can commit to being lifelong learners. I'm sure there are many others you are either practicing right now or can think of if you sit down and get creative. But the point is, never think you have all the answers or that you have nothing left to learn. Nothing could be further from the truth. That's not even the goal of a great leader. Rather, keep an open mind and an open spirit that says, "I want to learn more about how to deal with difficult and challenging situations." If you do this on a regular basis, you will be amazed at how those around you will offer advice and insight. Further, as smart as you are and as effective a leader as you may be, the feedback that you get is probably not going to be something you thought of or were aware of on your own. Funny, that's the way learning works. I know it has for me. I hope it continues to do that for you.

Pope Francis: A Leader Who Never Stopped Learning

Finally, we consider the case of one of the most admired leaders in the world today. Pope Francis is an extraordinary leader, but what is even more extraordinary is how he evolved and grew, with great effort, into the special leader he is today. The pope is admired by millions for his ability to connect with all kinds of people—of any age, Catholic or not, male or female—in virtually any country he visits. He is recognized for his humility and his humanity. He reminds us to be better as human beings and to be better to each other, particularly those who are suffering. He also seems open to different point of views, different opinions. Pope Francis says we need to be able to have conversations about things we disagree on, including the most sensitive and difficult subjects and issues that often divide us. These are many of the traits of a truly great leader.

Yet, Jorge Mario Bergoglio made lots of mistakes in the time between 1973 and 1990 in his role as a key leader of Catholic Jesuit priests in his home country of Argentina—a lofty position bestowed upon him by the Vatican. His leadership style rubbed many people the wrong way, and he has even called himself a "political animal."

In his first interview as pope, he reflected on his previous approach to dealing with others: "I had to deal with difficult situations, and I made my decisions abruptly and by myself. My authoritarian and quick manner of making decisions led me to have serious problems and to be accused of being ultra-conservative."[2]

By the time he ended his leadership role as rector of Buenos Aires's Jesuit seminary in 1986, after years of contention and strife, Bergoglio had lost the support of most of the Catholic priests who were his key stakeholders. According to Paul Vallely, in an article for *The Atlantic* titled, "Where the Pope Learned Humility": "Those who loathed him had begun to outnumber those who loved him. His support within the order had been eroded by his authoritarian style and his incorrigible inability, in the words of the Jesuit, Father Frank Brennan, 'to let go the reins of office once a [Jesuit] provincial of a different hue was in the saddle.' Another senior Jesuit explained: 'He drove people really crazy with his insistence that only he knew the right way to do things. Finally the other Jesuits said: 'Enough.'"[3]

Bergoglio was then banished by Rome and sent to a remote place called Cordoba. He was stripped of his leadership position as well as his many privileges and responsibilities. He couldn't even say Mass in a Jesuit church. The phone calls he made required permission from his superiors. Those who supported him in the past were advised not to deal with him directly. He was ostracized—totally. He was considered a leadership failure in a very public way. However, the man who would ultimately become pope could hear confession, and according to Vallely, "He spent a lot of time looking out the window and walking the streets, from the Jesuit residence to the church along a road that passed through many different areas of the city. People from all walks of life—academics, students, lawyers, and ordinary folk—visited the church for the penitential sacrament. He found his interactions with the poor particularly moving."

In the article, Vallely goes on to quote Father Guillermo Marco, who knew Bergoglio well and said, "Cordoba was, for Bergoglio, a place of humility and humiliation."[4] After two years in exile in Cordoba, Bergoglio returned as an auxiliary bishop in Buenos Aires.

To those who knew him, it was clear that in the time he was away, this future pope thought long and hard about the kind of leader he wanted to be and the kind of relationships he wanted to have with others. He decided that being an authoritarian leader wasn't the way to go. He learned to delegate more, listen to others, and engage in a more participatory approach to leadership and decision making. He also adopted a more humble philosophy to leadership and life. More humility. He acknowledged he didn't have all of the answers, that he wasn't all-knowing. He started asking others to pray for him, as he still does to this day.

It was twenty-three years ago that Bergoglio began this leadership transformation—dramatically changing his leadership style, his approach to being in charge and dealing with others. It is safe to say that if he hadn't done this—hadn't put in all the hard work necessary to learn and make these changes—he wouldn't have moved up the ranks and built the relationships necessary in the Catholic Church to eventually be elected pope and become the admired and revered leader that he is today. Who says you can't learn, particularly, later in your career? This pope did, and so can you. We can all learn and grow and ultimately improve to be the best leaders possible, especially if we decide that what we're doing currently isn't working or getting us to where we want to be, or helping us accomplish what we want to get done. Pope Francis is living proof of that.

19

Step Up and Take Responsibility, and Never Abandon the Ship

One of the most important things a leader can do is to step up and be accountable, be responsible, take the hit, stand up to the firestorm, and own it—all of it. No excuses, no caveats, no finger pointing, no scapegoating, no parsing of words or hiding behind lawyers or legal jargon. It's so rare these days—be it in politics, business, sports, or any professional arena—to see leaders truly taking responsibility or being accountable. When it does happen, it's worth celebrating and learning from because these lessons in leadership about responsibility teach us so much about ourselves and our character and who we truly are under pressure. It's funny: we tell our children so often that it's important to be responsible and just simply tell the truth about the mistakes they've made. Yet, as adults in leadership positions, we fail to live up to the same standard.

In my second book, *Make the Connection*, I shared the amazing story of Hank Keirsey, a military leader who demonstrated extraordinary leadership when he could have easily ducked responsibility and pinned the blame on others in his troop when things went seriously wrong. Let me recount what Keirsey did, which will put the other cases I share in this chapter in better context. My focus will be on cases of people in leadership positions who failed to do anything remotely comparable to what Hank Keirsey did.

Hank Keirsey Walked the Walk

In 1999, Lieutenant Colonel Keirsey's leadership was called into question when a West Point aviation captain by the name of Dan Dent created a PowerPoint presentation slide involving inappropriate homosexual humor. The crude attempt at poking fun at an inside joke among cadets was accidentally circulated, and the incident was immediately brought to the military powers that be. Dent, who had two small children and another on the way, was in deep trouble. What happened next demonstrates a critical lesson in leadership for us all. As Dent's commanding officer and the leader of so many others in Keirsey's troop at West Point, the lieutenant colonel decided to go to his superiors and take full responsibility for the incident and the mistake his subordinate had made.

Keirsey explained he did this because it was the right thing to do; he felt it was his duty as a leader to take responsibility for the actions of any member of his team. Further, he expected that as a military veteran he would probably get a slap on the wrist, as opposed to Captain Dent who would face much worse. Except that's not what happened. Despite twenty-four years of dedicated military service and an exemplary record of training thousands of young cadets in leadership at West Point, Lieutenant Colonel Keirsey was thrown out—discharged—with the following explanation: "LTC Keirsey . . . has created and fostered an environment in Military Training that is antithetical to Army values, professional standards, and the development of cadets into officers of character." The West Point community was stunned.[1]

Hank Keirsey took a bullet for one of his team members, the kind of bullet that ended a distinguished career in an instant. Dan Dent may have made the mistake, but Keirsey held himself personally and professionally responsible for this captain's actions.

Consider how rare this kind of leadership is in business, in government, in sports, or frankly, in everyday life. How many high-profile figures are quick to blame subordinates for things that go wrong? How many of our peers would point their finger at a lower-level associate without the blink of an eye? Scapegoating has become a leadership art form in today's workplace.

Sometimes being a great leader involves taking responsibility for the actions of someone on your team. Truly exceptional leadership is about sacrificing your personal and professional success for something larger. A lot of people talk the talk, but in a moment of truth, Lieutenant Colonel Hank Keirsey (ret.) walked the walk.

Now let me share some very different lessons of people in leadership positions who were anything but responsible and accountable when things went wrong and the pressure was on. We start with Tom Brady who knows the "blame game" very well.

Tom Brady "Deflates" His Credibility

For leaders, apologies can be a complex thing. Some leaders are convinced that apologizing is a sign of weakness or admission of guilt from which it is impossible to recover. In a conversation with NBC's Lestor Holt, when I appeared on the *Today Show* in May 2015 in connection with the so-called Deflategate controversy involving football star Tom Brady, I said that the New England Patriots quarterback was making a big mistake by refusing to apologize for any aspect of this thoroughly embarrassing and absurd situation. Keep in mind that Tom Brady is not only one of the most highly paid quarterbacks and professional athletes but also the unquestioned *leader* of his team.

When I spoke about Brady's mistakes on the *Today Show*, I wasn't referring to his ultimate guilt or innocence with respect to whether he himself directly told anyone to take air out of footballs in the AFC Championship to give him an advantage when throwing those footballs in such a critical game. Rather, I said that Brady should apologize at the very least for saying to some Patriots employees who had access to those footballs—be it implied or otherwise—that he wanted those footballs at a certain air pressure level lower than the official legal limit sanctioned by the NFL. I'm not sure if it was his lawyers or his PR advisors who told him not to apologize, but by refusing to do so he wound up taking no responsibility for any of this much publicized fiasco, which simply came down to cheating by giving his team an unfair advantage.

But what bothers me more is the clear lack of accountability Brady displayed following the release of Ted Wells's report for the NFL and throughout his handling—or lack thereof—of the situation. In an interview with sportscaster Jim Gray shortly after the release of the Wells report, Brady ducked and giggled and delivered a glib and sophomoric response to the conclusion that he, most likely, knew that the New England Patriots lower-level staff were deflating footballs to his liking in the AFC Championship game—clearly violating the rules. Further, in the interview with Gray, Brady said he had not read the NFL report and stated simply, "Usually I'm used to reading X's and O's and this was a little bit longer." The hometown New England audience laughed. Many others, who expect adults and leaders to take responsibility for their actions, were appalled. Brady's actions were disgraceful. He's supposed to be a role model to kids for how to play the game and how to win fairly.[2]

In the press conference before the Super Bowl, Brady bragged that he had never broken any rules in the NFL, while at the same time he was probably putting pressure and possibly directing the Patriots ball boys to break the rules for him. What kind of leader is that? The answer: one with very little courage and even less integrity. One who figures he can let someone way down in the organization take the hit while he stays above the fray.

What a powerful lesson in how *not* to lead. The NFL seemed to agree when they decided to punish Brady and the Patriots for their involvement in the Deflategate scandal, handing down a four-game suspension for Brady and a one-million-dollar fine to the Patriots in addition to two docked draft picks. Of course, Brady appealed the NFL's decision, again refusing to take responsibility for his involvement. Later, the federal judge who was ultimately responsible for hearing Brady's appeal would reverse the four-game suspension, only for the punishment to be reinstated following a series of further appeals. Yet, the ultimate legal ruling has no impact on Brady's failure as a leader in the case. Rather, it is a question of how a particular judge determined what penalty is appropriate in the case at hand. That's a legal issue. Leadership and responsibility comes down to a different equation.

Further, I suspect Brady will never admit he did, in fact, direct the Patriots staff to break the rules and deflate the footballs to his liking. As long as the Patriots are winning and Brady is playing well—no harm, no foul, in the minds of some. It is unlikely Brady will ever own up to his involvement and hold himself accountable as a leader and a role model. Some will say all this is much ado about nothing, with so many "real" issues going in the world. But this is not about football, it's about making sure our kids know that the old adage "It's how you play the game" really does matter and it's not just about winning or losing. Somewhere along the way, this great athlete forgot that lesson. What's worse, when he got caught, it seems he was dumb enough to try to cover it up and stick the blame on some low-level Patriots employee who was afraid to cross the golden boy with all those Super Bowl rings.

Yes, indeed, Tom Brady is a great athlete but a terrible leader—and, it appears, not a very nice person either. Maybe that's why Donald Trump is such a fan. (See my case study on Donald Trump later in this chapter for yet another example of leaders lacking the courage to take responsibility for their inexcusable actions.)

Yet, Tom Brady is not alone. Other athletes, like Alex Rodriguez, are famous for doing the same type of thing when it comes to the use of performance-enhancing drugs: not only refusing to apologize when first accused of using steroids but denying it publicly, slamming others, and then, ultimately, being *forced* to apologize after being caught red-handed and backed into a corner. A-Rod did all this after threatening to sue Major League Baseball and his own team, the Yankees, for challenging him on his use of steroids. At least A-Rod did eventually apologize, unlike home run king Barry Bonds and All-Star pitcher Roger Clemens. Both were steroid abusers, and both were role models to kids who look up to them and were considered leaders of their respective teams. Not only have Bonds and Clemens continued to deny ever using performance-enhancing drugs, but they've refused to apologize and of course blamed everyone else they could for their own actions.

The Cases of Clinton, Trump, and Rawlings-Blake

The world of sports is only one arena where such leadership flaws exist. Consider leaders in the world of politics, such as Hillary Clinton, who appears to have real difficulty when it comes to apologizing and taking responsibility for her mistakes. In fact, decades before Clinton's much publicized e-mail issues, it was her husband, Bill, then president of the United States, who refused to apologize for his sexual relationship with a twenty-one-year-old White House intern. Rather, his initial reaction was to hold a press conference and deny it—saying, "I did not have sex with that woman—Ms. Lewinski." Of course, Bill Clinton was lying. There was a sexual relationship. Monica Lewinski was a twenty-one-year-old intern; Bill Clinton was the president of the United States. And, in the end, after he was backed into a corner and the evidence came out, he had no choice but to apologize.

As for Hillary Clinton, as I write this chapter, she continues to be embroiled in a major controversy involving the alleged inappropriate use of a private e-mail server when she was secretary of state. For a federal official like Hillary Clinton, this was clearly against the spirit of a government policy that had been put in place, and may have risked the security and confidentiality of such e-mails dealing with sensitive world matters. Yet for nearly six months, she not only refused to apologize but adamantly stated she was the target of a partisan conspiracy and that she did nothing wrong. Both Hillary and Bill Clinton would go on the offensive and say that much of the e-mail controversy was a product of the media unfairly going after Mrs. Clinton, and of Republican disdain for the Clintons overall. Yet, as of this writing, Hillary Clinton finally apologized for this mistake in an interview with ABC News's David Muir, during which she said, "That was a mistake. I'm sorry about that. I take responsibility."[3]

To be clear, I'm not making a legal argument here, and this isn't about presidential politics, it's about Hillary Clinton as a leader who has made many tough decisions dealing with extremely difficult and sensitive matters but seems to have a very difficult time saying, "I screwed up" or "I was wrong. There is no excuse for why I was using a private e-mail account when I was secretary of state, and I apologize. It was a mistake and I need to do better in the future." For a strong leader, doing this upfront would have been the right thing to do. Yet, Clinton only apologized after being asked to do it countless times, when she was backed into a corner and her poll numbers were dropping daily. From my perspective, this approach is too late, it's too calculated, and it just doesn't seem genuine. Now, the fact that Clinton used a private e-mail account doesn't make her a terrible person, and I'm not convinced it makes her a terrible leader. It makes her a leader who made a stupid mistake, which she ought to admit. Join the club, Mrs. Clinton—a club all of us are in!

I'll tell you who else is in this club but refuses to acknowledge it: Donald Trump. While I have no idea how his presidential campaign will ultimately play out, or where Trump will stand when this book is published, I'm still amazed that someone with such obvious character and leadership flaws could be so popular with so many. Not only is he not a legitimate leader—by any reasonable standard of defining a leader—he's the king of childish and mean-spirited insults. Donald Trump is like the Don Rickles of presidential politics. He insults just about everyone. Except Rickles is funny; Trump is just mean. As Peter Wehner, a senior White House advisor to George W. Bush, once said, "He shouldn't be let near a Twitter account, let alone nuclear weapons."[4]

We're talking about someone who not only refused to apologize to Mexican immigrants for his outrageous and xenophobic comments after calling them "rapists," but rather he doubled down by bragging that his comments on illegal immigration caused him to rise in the polls. As if saying offensive, outrageous, and factually incorrect things is okay as long as enough other people agree with it. That's not leadership—that's demagoguery.

What really concerns me about Donald Trump—the guy who said he should be America's next leader—is his unwillingness or inability to take responsibility when things go wrong; instead, he blames others. Yet, he wants all the credit when things are glitzy and glamorous and The Donald can be The Donald. To me, the value of a brand that you can count on is largely a product of how the leader, much less the namesake of the brand, stands up or doesn't when things go wrong. If you're going to put your name on everything, not just casinos and buildings, but TV shows, water bottles, golf courses, and shirts at those golf courses (his golf courses are, in fact, first rate), among other things—(Trump also put his name on a university, Trump University, which was shut down and is mired in lawsuits by students who said they got ripped off by Trump after the Better Business Bureau gave Trump University an absolutely terrible independent evaluation)—real leaders must take responsibility when things go wrong for organizations they are so closely tied to or when their name is slapped all over it.[5]

Yes, Trump is great showman. He's a super self-promoter. He's great for those of us in the media looking for red meat and outrageous sound bites from a political candidate. But he's no real leader. He's a carnival barker. He's the former host of a celebrity reality show that set up conflict and drama simply so that, in a highly produced setting, he could look into the camera and tell a contestant, "You're fired!" That's not leadership. That's TV production. That's show business. That's entertainment. Real leadership is about owning your mistakes. It's about saying responsible things on the campaign trail and, when you don't or you otherwise screw up, admitting it, rather than blaming others when they criticize you. It's about having humility and the confidence to apologize when you have clearly said something that is outrageously offensive, which we all know he does often.

Remember the Republican debate on Fox News in August 2015? A very important leadership lesson played out when Fox News anchor Megyn Kelly simply asked Donald Trump, then the leading GOP candidate, to explain his grotesque and totally unacceptable past descriptions of women, including "fat pigs," "dogs," "slobs," and "disgusting animals." Ever the showman, Trump tried to duck responsibility at first with a snarky one-liner, saying he was only talking about Rosie O'Donnell—as if that would make it acceptable.[6] When Kelly pressed him on the fact that this simply wasn't true, Trump—who never takes responsibility for his comments or actions (a terrible leadership trait)—launched into an absurd diatribe about political correctness and then accused Kelly of not being nice to him and threatened to be "not nice" to her for simply asking him a direct question about something he didn't want to talk about.

Later, when confronted with his own words, Trump demonstrated his lack of leadership again and again by refusing to simply apologize for his grotesque use of language and for offending so many people. Trump has come to the conclusion that somehow apologizing makes him appear less of an alpha male or a strong leader when, in fact, the exact opposite is true. True leadership is about having the confidence and the emotional intelligence to know that you simply made a stupid mistake or said the wrong thing and need to own what you've done. As of this writing, Trump can't and won't do that, which by itself should disqualify him from having any real leadership responsibilities.

Again, while it is unclear how the presidential race will play out as I write this chapter, the lesson in leadership is obvious. Being the leader of the free world is not like running a reality show. It's not Celebrity Apprentice. It's not a Trump-sponsored beauty contest or golf event. We are talking about real life, and real leadership involving very real problems, because every life matters and there is so much at stake for our country. As I have said before, Donald Trump is no leader, but his type of public leader is very dangerous. As leaders, Donald Trump reminds us that we must take responsibility not only for our actions but also for our words, especially when things go wrong.

Another case of a leader who failed to hold herself accountable for slip of the tongue is Baltimore mayor Stephanie Rawlings-Blake.

As she attempted to handle the riots on the streets of Baltimore following the funeral of Freddie Gray, businesses were being destroyed, police officers were being attacked, and so-called protesters acted like thugs on the street engaging in lawless looting, burning, and pillaging of their community. The reasons for what happened in Baltimore are complex. Yet, there is a clear lesson in leadership in all of this. Not only did it take far too long for the leaders of Baltimore to reach out to the state and, ultimately, the federal government for help, but they clearly were not prepared for what happened.

Further, Mayor Rawlings-Blake, mishandled the situation when she spoke in public and uttered these shocking words: "It's a very delicate balancing act, because while we tried to make sure that they [protesters] were protected from the cars and the other things that were going on, we also gave those who wished to destroy space to do that as well."[7] This clearly sent the wrong message to those looking to cause harm and do damage in Baltimore.

Talk about lessons in leadership. Those in positions of authority must choose their words in a crisis and under pressure very carefully. The mayor said absolutely the wrong thing, sending the wrong message. When challenged about her statement, she pushed back hard in a defensive tone saying; "I never said, nor would I ever say that we are giving people space to destroy our city. So my words should not be twisted."[8] But that excuse doesn't cut it for a real leader. She said it; she has to own it. The mayor was not responsible for the lawlessness on the streets of Baltimore, but she clearly contributed to it by her careless public comment. By not taking responsibility for her words, she demonstrated exceptionally poor leadership and only compounded a bad situation.

As leaders, we all make mistakes, especially under heavy pressure. But when we do, and things go wrong, we have only one choice—to step up and be the responsible adult and say, "I was wrong for saying what I did. I apologize. What I should have said was . . . ." By making excuses and playing the victim, Mayor Rawlings-Blake sent the wrong message again to those in Baltimore and around the country looking to make excuses for the criminals—no matter how young they are—wreaking havoc on the streets of Baltimore. Now, that is a lesson in leadership.

Never Abandon the Ship

Finally, being accountable is not always a matter of simply apologizing for mistakes or for your words. Sometimes the situation is worse, and leaders are in a position, when they screw up, to put the lives of others on the line. To understand the gravity of such situations, consider the captain of the massive cruise liner *Costa Concordia* and the tragic events that occurred on January 13, 2012.

Several years ago, the *Costa Concordia* luxury cruise ship was on the first leg of a cruise around the Mediterranean Sea carrying more than 4,000 passengers and crew. As the ship passed the Tuscan island of Giglio, Italy, the ship deviated from its planned route, coming closer to the island, and ultimately struck a rock formation on the sea floor. The impact could be heard by passengers on board and caused a temporary power blackout when water flooded the engine room. Yet, the ship's captain failed to order an evacuation until after an hour of drifting, at which point it was believed he was already safely on shore.

It was initially believed that the ship's captain, Francesco Schettino, took the cruise liner off course to wave to a former colleague, in what many called a reckless show of bravado. Schettino would later admit in a court proceeding that his reason for sailing so close to Giglio—leading the ship to hit rocks—was to "impress the passengers."[9] Yet, this act of "showboating" that caused the ship to take on water was not the captain's worst leadership act. Rather, it was his actions following this critical mistake that offer all of us a lesson in what *not* to do when things go seriously wrong and others whom you are responsible for are at risk. Schettino fled. He abandoned the ship! He left the passengers aboard the sinking vessel to fend for themselves. But even after Schettino abandoned the ship and refused to go back, he refused to take responsibility and own the decision he made. He not only "lawyered up," he spun the story, saying in court as well as in the public media, "I was trying to get people to get into the boats in an orderly fashion. Suddenly, since the ship was at a 60 to 70 [degree] angle, I tripped, and I ended up in one of the boats. That's how I found myself in the lifeboat."[10]

However, transcripts of calls between Captain Schettino and the coast guard tell a very different story. According to these radio transmissions, a top port authority official repeatedly berated Schettino for not returning to the ship, telling him, "Captain, this is an order, now I am in charge. Get back on that ship and coordinate the operations. There are already casualties." The captain responded, "How many?" to which the official exclaimed, "You should tell me that! What do you want to do, go home? Now you get back on that ship and tell us what can be done, how many people are still there and what do they need."[11] The captain nevertheless refused to go back on the sinking ship.

Thirty-two passengers died that day, and after a turbulent nineteen-month trial, a three-judge panel found Schettino guilty of several charges, including manslaughter. Yet, Captain Schettino maintained his innocence and refused to acknowledge that any of his cowardly actions had taken place. So not only did this leader abandon the ship to save his own hide—after he arrogantly put the ship in risk—he refused to admit that he had done anything wrong. Instead he clutched at excuses and went as far as to say he was the victim of the media that needed a "scapegoat."[12]

There are many leadership lessons we can learn from the *Costa Concordia* disaster. There are issues regarding preparation for a disaster as well as how to handle a crisis in a calm, composed, and clear-headed fashion. But the biggest lesson in leadership is the most obvious one: that a captain—in this case, Captain Francesco Schettino—should never abandon his ship.

Yes, this is about a literal ship, but the same lesson is true in any organization. You don't abandon your ship. You don't turn your back on the people who depend on you for their safety and well-being—whether they are your employees or your most valued stakeholders. There are also important lessons here for the rest of us the next time something goes seriously wrong when we are at the helm.

- It's not a matter of *if* something goes wrong but a matter of *when*, because something inevitably *will* go wrong. There are too many variables. Stuff happens. While you can't think of every conceivable scenario where a disaster or crisis could occur, it is important that before one does, you not only identify the most likely circumstances but also have a plan that is realistic and practical to deal with it. A leader's job is to ensure that while all precautions are taken, the preparation for a crisis never stops.

- Great leaders never underestimate how bad a situation is by engaging in wishful thinking. They always consider the worst-case scenario when something goes wrong. It's not a matter of being negative or pessimistic, but rather of asking yourself, "If the worst happens, what do I and my team need to do?" Clearly Schettino didn't do this. Instead, he communicated to the over 4,000 people on the ship that there was some sort of electrical problem and that there was no reason to be overly concerned. Again, this was wishful thinking or an outright lie. I'm not advocating that you talk to people in a fashion that produces hysteria and panic, but rather you show a degree of candor about the severity of the situation and the need to be calm and deliberate in your actions.

- It is clear there were few, if any, leaders on the *Costa Concordia* staff who were in a position to take charge or give clear directions once Captain Schettino abandoned ship. Great leadership isn't only for those at the top of the organization; it is required throughout a team. We have to question whether Schettino or the *Costa Concordia* executive team developed any other "situational" leaders who were positioned to do what needed to be done in case of a crisis or emergency in which Schettino wouldn't or couldn't lead. Even in the best circumstances, no one leader can do it alone. He or she needs others to help execute in a crisis.

- Great leaders don't panic. They have a sense of calm, even in the most dangerous and perilous situation. We saw it during 9/11 with the crew and passengers of Flight 93 that crashed into a field in rural Pennsylvania. We saw it with Captain Chesley Sullenberger, known as "Sully," the pilot of the US Airways plane that landed in the Hudson River. His calm demeanor had a direct impact on the demeanor of others around him. Conversely, when a leader panics, it is inevitable that he or she will induce panic in others.

There are many lessons in leadership that all of us can learn from the *Costa Concordia* tragedy, as well as from the leadership shortcomings of others discussed in this chapter. So the next time something goes wrong when you are in charge, remember, great leaders step up and take responsibility. Anything less is unacceptable and only makes a difficult situation worse.

20

Leadership Lessons from JFK

One of the best and most profound presidential lessons in leadership emanated from the failure of the 1961 invasion of the Bay of Pigs. It was clearly President John F. Kennedy's most significant and embarrassing public failure in his three years as president. Many leaders would have found it extremely difficult, if not impossible, to recover from such a devastating defeat. The Bay of Pigs fiasco was a three-day battle that began on April 17, 1961. As our commander-in-chief, Kennedy made the fateful decision to take the advice of top military leaders and allow approximately 1,400 "Cuban exiles," who were supported by American military training and equipment, to invade what was known as the Bay of Pigs in Cuba. American military personnel were also involved.

The plan was for the group to gain the support of disillusioned Cubans who would join the effort to overthrow President Fidel Castro, except that as the world would come to find out, it didn't work out that way. Castro's forces of more than 20,000 military troops were waiting, and they ultimately captured and killed many of the invading force, including several Americans. The United States was publicly embarrassed, and Castro scoffed at Kennedy, who immediately regretted his decision to invade. The event was viewed by many as a presidential leadership failure that, on the unforgiving international cold-war stage, was near fatal for JFK.

Weeks after this debacle, Kennedy told reporter Hugh Sidey, who later wrote about this conversation for a *Time* magazine story on April 16, 2001: "I want to know how all this could have happened. There were 50 or so of us, presumably the most experienced and smartest people we could get, to plan such an operation. . . . But five minutes after it began to fall in, we all looked at each other and asked, 'How could we have been so stupid?' . . . I guess you get walled off from reality when you want something to succeed too much."[1]

But Kennedy was a quick learner and used the lessons from the Bay of Pigs to bring a peaceful resolution to the pressure-filled, high-stakes Cuban Missile Crisis in 1962. Some of those same leadership mistakes and lessons are just as relevant today, not only for a president of the United States, but for any leader facing a challenging and complicated set of obstacles. Consider the following:

- Leaders must aggressively challenge all advice or recommendations, regardless of the source, and assume the potential for the worst-case scenario. After the Bay of Pigs, JFK acknowledged that he did not challenge the military leaders around him who were convinced the mission would work. As leaders, we often assume or convince ourselves that the best-case scenario is likely, a risky approach at best. By assuming the worst-case scenario, strong leaders can prepare for contingencies—other options. Or they can ask, "So what do we do if our plan does not work or we are attacked by our opposition?" Further, by challenging even the best and brightest advisors around them, there is the potential to generate a fuller, more honest, and much-needed debate. When leaders challenge those around them with probing tough questions, they are often able to get better, more accurate information about complex and multifaceted situations. In the process, they also raise the bar as well as the expectations for the team around them. If Kennedy had done this in connection with the misguided Bay of Pigs invasion, he might have made different decisions, which, in turn, could have changed the course of history in U.S., Cuban, and Soviet relations—given the events of the Cuban Missile Crisis less than a year after the Bay of Pigs incident.

- Great leaders must create an environment where the opportunity for team members to challenge them is encouraged and supported. Historical accounts after the Bay of Pigs fiasco indicate that many advisors in the Kennedy inner circle were opposed to invading Cuba but kept silent. In fact, CIA director Allen Dulles was aware that Cuban president Fidel Castro—whom President Kennedy appears to have been obsessed with overthrowing—had approximately 200,000 troops at his disposal. This is compared with the 1,400 inexperienced Cuban volunteers who were to be supported by a very limited U.S. Air Force operation. While some Kennedy insiders and members of Congress aware of the Bay of Pigs operation later said they had serious misgivings about its chances for success, there are few, if any, historical accounts of President Kennedy's receiving significant pushback, or even information or intelligence about the operation—including from CIA director Dulles—that would have given the president reason to pause.

As I mentioned earlier, President Kennedy, when speaking about the Bay of Pigs operation, told Sidey, "I guess you get walled off from reality when you want something too much."[2] We've all been there as leaders. We become too tied to a particular goal or outcome, and we lose our objectivity. Our judgment can become compromised and clouded. It can send the message to those around us that we only want information and advice that reinforces our point of view. Further, if no one is playing devil's advocate, the risk of engaging in groupthink with yes players is dangerous and can lead to deadly consequences. During the Cuban Missile Crisis of 1962, which was ultimately resolved successfully, several options for resolution were put on the table. In the Bay of Pigs, only one option was considered—the invasion of Cuba. Kennedy clearly learned that it is essential for leaders to have multiple options available for debate and discussion.

Additional lessons learned by President Kennedy in connection with the Bay of Pigs fiasco that offer tips and tools for other leaders facing pressure-filled situations include the following:

- Wise leaders must be wary of overconfidence bordering on cockiness or arrogance. It seems JFK, and his team of advisors, were convinced that by simply having U.S. military forces involved—even in a limited fashion—victory in Cuba was highly likely, if not assured. This mindset may have caused President Kennedy to underestimate Fidel Castro and his ability to respond to the U.S.-backed initiative. An important lesson for any leader is to never underestimate your competition, regardless of how things may appear "on paper." Your opponent's will and desire to compete or fight against you in any arena can and often does change the equation.

- As I also discuss in chapter 19, no matter how bad a mistake a leader makes, or whoever else was involved in the decision-making process, truly great leaders step up and own it. According to Ralph Martin's book, *A Hero for Our Time,* after the Bay of Pigs debacle, Defense Secretary Robert McNamara recommended that responsibility be shared among many in the administration, saying, "We could have recommended against it and we didn't." To which President Kennedy responded, "Absolutely not. I am the president. I could have decided otherwise. It is my responsibility."[3] Great leaders step up and take responsibility when things go wrong—even when given the option to spread the blame or pass the buck.

Finally, in the spirit of this book, Gary Burnison, chief executive officer at Korn/Ferry International and LinkedIn Influencer, says of JFK and the Bay of Pigs: "To be an effective leader, you must demonstrate learning agility—the ability to learn from experience and apply that learning to new, first-time situations. For Kennedy, probably a great and painful learning lesson was the Bay of Pigs—a botched attempt to oust Fidel Castro from power in Cuba. Under the President's direction, the mission was undermanned. The failed attempt led to death of the invaders."[4]

Kennedy chronicler Hugh Sidey has also shared what JFK's father, Ambassador Joseph P. Kennedy, said to him about his son's leadership experience in connection with the Bay of Pigs: "I tell you, Hugh, Jack is the luckiest guy I know. He could fall into a pile of manure and come up smelling like a rose. The Bay of Pigs and the other things were the best lesson he could have gotten and he got them all early. He knows what will work and what won't, who he can trust and who he can't, who will stick with him and who will not." Says Sidey, "Old Joe was right. Kennedy stood up to it, took the blame for the Bay of Pigs, rearranged his staff, and a year later when confronted by the Cuban Missile Crisis steered a steady and successful course through that nuclear peril."[5]

More than half a century later, leaders continue to face pressure-filled situations, and the powerful leadership lessons cited in this chapter about JFK and the Bay of Pigs are more relevant than ever before.

21

Leadership and *The Godfather*

A Lesson You Can't Refuse

Like so many fans who are a bit obsessed with *The Godfather* movies (I and II, but definitely not III), I find myself quoting Francis Ford Coppola's cinematic masterpiece in numerous situations. I've had endless trivia contests and challenges about one-liners and scenes from *The Godfather* with my close friend and lawyer Nick Grieco, as well as other "*Godfather* experts." It's one thing to quote Pete Clemenza, the loyal and ruthless soldier of Don Vito Corleone, following a pivotal murder scene when he tells his accomplice Rocco, "Leave the gun. Take the cannoli." It is, however, quite another to analyze *The Godfather* on a deeper level. I'm talking about examining the complex and conflicted relationships between rivals (such as Jewish mob leader Hyman Roth and other mob associates) as well as how an effective leader deals with difficult and thorny situations and circumstances. For example, what should Don Vito's prodigal son, Michael, do once he realizes that his own brother, Fredo, betrayed him, thereby putting Michael's life in danger?

I have often said that many of the challenges I have faced as a leader can be looked at or put in context by one scene or quotation or another from *The Godfather*. But sometimes my colleagues—who aren't *Godfather*-obsessed—are perplexed when I make these references, not really understanding why I see *The Godfather* as a useful metaphor for leadership and life. With this in mind, I describe some of the most significant leadership lessons from *The Godfather*.

- "Keep your friends close, but your enemies closer." This is what Don Vito Corleone says to his cohorts with respect to whom he could trust and whom he couldn't as he was expanding his criminal power base and was concerned about the prospect of betrayal and treachery. Often, as leaders, we put the people we deal with into two distinct categories, our supporters and our detractors—or, simply put, our "friends" and our "enemies." The problem for many leaders, whether the head of a large corporation, a baseball coach, or a hospital CEO, is that we gravitate almost exclusively to people we get along with and like. It's natural. It's human nature. Yet, Don Vito offers valuable leadership insight by reminding us to never assume our "friends" or those we simply like will stay loyal or supportive. He advises that we work to "keep them close" and to let them know how important and valuable they are to us.

  Further, Corleone reminds us that taking our friends for granted is risky business indeed. As leaders, when we do this we allow our so-called friends to feel slighted and unimportant. Whether these are our clients, our employees, our peers, or our vendors, we risk the potential for them to feel used. Being taken for granted can cause these friends to feel taken advantage of, to be de-motivated and, possibly, less loyal to us when the chips are down and things are not going well for us personally or for our organization. Further, not keeping friends "close" may tempt them to align with our competitors or, dare I say, enemies who could seize the opportunity to entice away our talented friends who simply aren't "feeling the love" from us.

  But what exactly is meant by "keeping your enemies closer"? In business, or in any professional endeavor where competition is part of the game, it is essential to identify and be aware of those who you believe have the potential to hurt you. You may be inclined to ignore them or fight them; sometimes these leadership strategies make the most sense. However, there are times when it is essential for leaders to stay connected to their so-called enemies by engaging them and interacting with them. Why do this? For many reasons, but the biggest is that by connecting with them on this level, you have the potential to learn what they're thinking and *why* they're thinking it.

Further, if you try to keep them "close," you also have the potential to neutralize their animosity toward you by finding common ground and areas of agreement or mutual interest that you never would have known about if you simply kept them at a distance at all times. When someone you haven't enjoyed a positive professional relationship with experiences a very public success or receives a significant award, what does it cost you as a leader—or just as a person—to send a note or an e-mail, or actually place a call of congratulations? Even if you wind up leaving a message and the other person doesn't respond, this effort to break the ice can go a long way toward opening the door that has been closed between you and a so-called enemy in business. Even if it simply makes the other person think twice before he takes an action that could potentially be harmful to you and your organization, it's worth it. The key for you as a leader is to maintain contact with the people in your professional orbit who could potentially be hurtful to you and to those around you. This takes a degree of confidence and maturity on the part of the leader to let go of a real or perceived vendetta that will ultimately go nowhere at best and at worst, has the potential to exacerbate an already unhealthy situation.

The same lesson applies when you consider your relationship with peers or colleagues who you can clearly say are not your enemies; yet, you wouldn't necessarily call your "friends." While you may be required to work with these folks in your department or perhaps interact with them in the same industry network, you know these people wouldn't go out of their way to help you and further, wouldn't think twice about pointing the finger of blame your way to save their own skin. These relationships are delicate. You must work at them. Think about it. You may never be this "frenemy's" favorite person; yet, by making an effort to keep such an individual "close" you can certainly get them to think more positively about you. Take the time to get to know them. Remember, it is easier to hurt someone professionally whom you don't interact with very much than the person you have connected with on a personal level, even if only in some small way. The closer you are, the harder it will be for them to "hurt you" if given the chance.

In addition, in a constantly changing world where mergers and acquisitions are the norm and clearly not the exception, your so-called enemy today may very easily wind up being someone (because of market forces) you are forced to be friends or at least colleagues with tomorrow. Leaders don't have the luxury to simply discount or ignore their enemies because it's the easier path to take. The world is too complex and relationships too dynamic to take such a simplistic leadership stance. Truly great leaders understand that who they like or don't like on a personal level and who they may naturally be friendly with does not dictate who they as leaders deal with or don't deal with. So "keep your friends close, but your enemies closer." It's a leadership lesson that works, regardless of whether you're talking about organized crime or the business of healthcare.

- "Never tell anyone outside the family what you're thinking." Yes, this is what Don Vito told his outspoken and often volatile son, Sonny Corleone, who had a habit of saying whatever came to mind in meetings with other organized crime families and associates. This would ultimately contribute to Sonny's being gunned down in a particularly brutal scene in *Godfather I*, but the larger point is about leaders having discretion, being disciplined, holding their tongue at critical moments in meetings and public situations, and not simply blurting out whatever they are thinking. It's not enough for a leader to say "It's the truth" as an explanation for why one says something. A statement being "the truth" is only part of a much more complex equation as to why some things should be said and others shouldn't, as well as *how* it should be said and in front of whom.

Now, I'm not advocating that Vito Corleone's leadership lesson about playing your cards very close to the vest should be taken to the extreme point where you never put your cards on the table or speak candidly and openly with others. However, he makes an important point for leaders, particularly in the age of social media, to not be such an open book and have what I like to call "diarrhea of the mouth." Another reason this shoot-from-the-lip leadership approach is particularly dangerous is because, when you say these particularly blunt and sometimes shocking things, the people you're speaking to might wonder whether you will repeat what they believe has been said in confidence. The key here is that leaders can be candid, direct, and honest while remaining disciplined, diplomatic, and selective in how they share information and still be highly successful.

- "You're not a wartime consigliere." This quote is about Tom Hagen, Sonny Corleone's stepbrother, who makes a difficult decision at a critical point in *The Godfather I* as it becomes clear that the Corleone family is about to engage in a violent war with other organized crime factions. While Tom has been a loyal soldier and smart advisor to whom Sonny shows nothing but love and affection (the brothers' father, Vito, took Tom in when he was abandoned as a small boy on the streets of New York), Sonny also realizes, when his father has just been shot in an assassination attempt and lies near death in a hospital bed, that the stakes have changed dramatically. The game has also changed. According to Sonny, who becomes the de facto leader of the Corleone family at this point, since Michael had only recently returned home, the situation required a different type of advisor: a "wartime consigliere."

Under these conditions, Sonny concluded that Tom lacked both the skill and the temperament to effectively perform in this role. In the movie, Sonny was killed soon thereafter and Tom ultimately maintained his important position in the Corleone family; however, the overarching point remains. The well-rounded leader understands that sometimes difficult decisions must be made regarding whom to put in certain positions and whom to remove from others in order for the organization to succeed. Often, making these decisions may hurt those you are closest to and offend the feelings of others. Many will question your motives and ask how you could do this to certain employees who have been so loyal and dedicated.

Yet, the exceptional leader understands that loyalty and dedication—while extremely important—are not the totality of what is required in certain positions at certain times. Rather, other skills involving strategic thinking, temperament, personality, and a range of other factors are highly relevant and must be considered. The leader who doesn't consider these factors and simply keeps people in place because of "their loyalty and dedication," much less because of history or bloodlines, is not an exceptional leader. While this leader's motives are understandable, sometimes an organization under extremely difficult, challenging, and extreme circumstances will, in fact, need a "wartime consigliere."

So, while *The Godfather* is largely about illegal criminal activities that are clearly deplorable, it is also about family, loyalty, business, competition, and how human beings interact and deal with each other in difficult, challenging, and sometimes complex and complicated situations. It is simplistic to say that the things that happen to the people in *The Godfather* are only relevant to organized crime during that period of America history. As Hyman Roth said in the film as he stood on a balcony in Havana, where he and his associates gathered to celebrate their success in the pre-Castro country that had opened its arms to organized crime, "We're bigger than U.S. Steel." That quote always stuck with me. The larger question is really whether being a leader and having what it took to succeed in an organized crime organization was all that much different than succeeding as a leader at "U.S. Steel" or a variety of other multinational and mega corporations. My point here is that business outside of organized crime is sometimes ugly, dirty, nasty, and dangerous. Leaders who don't understand this, and who are not effective in navigating these shark-infested waters, will never truly succeed for themselves or for their organization. This is exactly why I find some of the leadership lessons from *The Godfather* to be absolutely relevant, not only in my career as a leader but also in my coaching and consulting work with other leaders in every professional arena.

22

Leadership Lessons from Lincoln

Abraham Lincoln was one of the great presidents in American history. While the movie *Lincoln*, released in 2012, got significant praise and shares much about the life of the sixteenth U.S. president, there is still much to learn and understand about how Lincoln led and how he came to be the leader who changed the course of our country and saved the Union.

Lincoln's leadership traits have stood the test of time and, while not perfect as a leader, he demonstrated the following characteristics (many of which are discussed throughout this book) from which all of us can continue to learn:

- Keep your enemies close. No—what Lincoln teaches us is not exactly what we learned from Don Vito Corleone in the movie *The Godfather* discussed in chapter 21 of this book. Yet, while most presidents throughout American history have surrounded themselves with a team of allies in an effort to form an inner circle of protection, Lincoln did not see leadership this way. Rather, he was confident enough in himself to create an inner circle of rivals who were among his worst enemies at an earlier time. Some of these same men, particularly William Henry Seward (who was Lincoln's main rival in 1860 and later became his secretary of state), wound up being some of Lincoln's most trusted advisers.

What a powerful leadership lesson. Many leaders surround themselves with people they are closest to on a personal level, or who have been part of their inner circle for years—often people who simply tell them what they want to hear—and are not secure enough to bring in other strong leaders, much less previous rivals. This myopic and ineffective approach increases the odds that only certain points of view will be heard, which can have a negative impact on the quality of the decisions ultimately reached. By turning to those who have a different point of view to help make decisions, as Lincoln did, leaders promote a more balanced, open-minded approach to leadership. This strategy also allows leaders to explore other points of view and opinions that they may never have considered and spurs debate and conversation, which ultimately increases the potential for a more well-rounded decision to be made.

• Find common ground. I recently reread the book *Team of Rivals* by Pulitzer Prize–winning author Doris Kearns Goodwin, one of the most comprehensive books about Lincoln and his extraordinary leadership ability. Consider the following passage, which recalls Lincoln's ability to build relationships when many lesser leaders would have failed: "His personal qualities enabled him to form friendships with men who had previously opposed him; to repair injured feelings that, left untended, might have escalated into permanent hostility; to assume responsibility for the failures of subordinates, to share credit with ease, and to learn from mistakes."[1] Goodwin's book and other historical accounts of Lincoln are filled with examples of how Lincoln consistently worked to find common ground with those whom opposed him. As I discuss in another chapter of this book, leadership is extremely personal, and a great lesson is to seek to find what you have in common with others—even if on the surface there appears to be little or nothing.

Finding this common ground is critical when you need to work with others to accomplish important things—which all leaders need to do. Further, finding common ground allows you to connect on a more personal and human level with others who may have opposed you on policy or substance. Interestingly, Ronald Reagan, a president I never considered an exceptional leader, seemed to have a Lincolnesque ability as a Republican president in the 1980s to find common ground with Congressman Tip O'Neill, a liberal Democrat from Massachusetts. Both were Irish. Both loved sports. Both loved to tell stories. It was this personal connection between Reagan and O'Neill that allowed them to work together in ways that are often odd or unlikely at our nation's capital, particularly among members of opposing political parties. Lincoln would have approved. Yet, finding common ground requires the desire to do so. You have to understand its importance and be willing to put time and effort into the process. Wanting to find common ground is one thing—actually finding it is a lot harder. But the payoff for leaders can be huge.

- Take responsibility. Lincoln demonstrated the Harry Truman leadership philosophy of "the buck stops here" on a regular basis. Too many leaders are caught up in playing the "blame game" when things go wrong, while Lincoln saw mistakes made by those on his team as ultimately his responsibility. We have seen countless examples of CEOs and other leaders not accepting responsibility for something that has gone wrong in their own organization. No matter if they were directly involved in a situation or not, they must step up, be a strong leader, and take responsibility. The key takeaway, as another chapter in this book explains, is that leaders who actually step up and take responsibility when things go wrong are often seen as stronger, more effective leaders than those who don't. Yet the leaders who can't or won't accept responsibility when things go wrong often say one of the main reasons they do this is because they don't want to be seen as weak or flawed. How ironic.

- Be self-aware. By most accounts, Lincoln was extremely self-aware. Goodwin argues that Lincoln had the potential to have serious mood shifts.[2] Like many leaders, he could get angry, but he had the uncanny ability to understand that the way he showed his anger toward those around him was critical to his success. For example, when Lincoln was particularly angry, he had a habit of writing a letter to the person he was angry with and then setting it aside. When he did verbally communicate his anger, he would quickly try to resolve the situation, refusing to allow unresolved conflict to fester. A leader must be a "leader of himself," which requires not only the Lincolnesque self-control described by Goodwin but also a level of self-awareness and, yes, "emotional intelligence," a concept discussed in greater detail in this book. While emotional intelligence was not a term or concept in vogue in the 1860s, Lincoln apparently understood how his inner moods and emotions affected his leadership style, which was critical to his success.

In my consulting work as an executive leadership coach, I often ask my clients to assess their own leadership strengths as well as the areas they need to improve. In many cases there is a significant disconnect between how my clients see themselves and their leadership skills and how they are seen by those who know them best. This inability to see or understand how our professional colleagues view us is problematic on many levels and seriously hurts our ability as leaders to improve and grow in critical areas.

- Display a strong sense of principles. One of Lincoln's other great leadership traits was his sense of integrity coupled with his strong belief in his principles. This is not a skill or a tool but rather a question of character. Obviously, Lincoln was willing to compromise. However, those around him could be confident his core principles would not change from day to day depending upon the circumstances around him or his perceived popularity at the time. Such leadership inspires the loyalty, dedication, and confidence of those around you. Too often we hear about politicians and other leaders who "flip-flop" on issues, depending on public opinion. True leaders stand firm and do not let outside influences change their core values. When leaders are so quick to compromise on their core principles in the name of expediency, there is little reason for the people they deal with to trust them when things get especially difficult or challenging. When leaders focus on self-preservation above all else, they will fail to engender the loyalty of key stakeholders needed to achieve great things.

Consider another account of Lincoln's leadership acumen and a true display of his commitment to principles. According to Steven Smith, in his article "What Sort of Leader Was Lincoln?," as late as the summer of 1864, Lincoln fully expected to be a one-term president. Even those within his own party were urging another candidate. And yet, he was the country's most important leader during the Civil War. Should the election be postponed, as some were proposing? On this point, Lincoln was in firm opposition. Suspending elections, even in the midst of war, was wrong, even if holding the election would have resulted in Lincoln's defeat and therewith the cause of the Union. "This morning, as for some days past," Lincoln wrote in a memorandum some time before the election, "It seems exceedingly probable that this Administration will not be re-elected. Then it will be my duty to so co-operate with the President elect, as to save the Union between the election and the inauguration; as he will have secured his election on such ground that he cannot possibly save it afterwards."[3]

To his credit, Lincoln realized that free elections should not, even in principle, be sacrificed even if the cost might be the end of constitutional government. For constitutional leadership, the ends do not justify the means. Constitutional leadership is necessarily limited or bounded leadership. It is in this possibility of a leader operating within the limits of constitutional restraint that the hope of our republic rests.[4] This issue of leadership and trust is more fully explored in chapter 12. Check it out for another valuable lesson in leadership.

- Demonstrate authenticity and genuineness. Lincoln's interpersonal skills were clearly a key to his success as a leader. Yet, he was not a slick or even a great public speaker. Again, being a great leader doesn't require that you have spectacular oratorical skills, yet you must be an exceptional overall communicator. Interestingly, Lincoln refused to speak in public without a prepared text. However, one of Lincoln's greatest gifts as a leader was that most people believed that he believed what he was saying when he spoke. In many ways, that is where the expression "Honest Abe" came from. An enduring leadership lesson: when people believe that you believe, it speaks volumes about your ability as a leader to get them to follow you.

The lesson here is to work to determine not just *what* you want to say but *why* you want to say it. Lincoln worked really hard, and often struggled, to figure out where he stood on key topics and then worked to find the words to get his message across. This is a task no great leader can delegate to a PR person or speechwriter. Yes, Abraham Lincoln offers many valuable lessons in leadership that remain as relevant and useful today as ever.

23

Obama as a Leader

You've Gotta Be More Engaged

Assessing President Barack Obama as a leader isn't easy. Mostly, it's because the job of being president of the United States, leader of the free world, often seems near impossible. Who am I, or rather, who is anyone—no matter how many books or articles you've written or courses and seminars you've taught on leadership—to judge a U.S. president as a leader? Yet, examining President Obama's leadership file offers some important leadership lessons for all of us that apply to any profession.

Interestingly, Barack Obama came to the office of the presidency with very little executive or leadership experience. As a legislator, he was a U.S. senator for a very brief time and was a state senator in Illinois before that. He also taught law at the University of Chicago. Previously, Obama was a community organizer. Yet, he never really ran a community organization as a CEO, was never a leader of a business or the head of a nonprofit. Further, while he served in government before becoming president, he was never a governor, which again means he never held an executive post.

So in many ways, Barack Obama's move to the presidency was a huge step up in leadership and, while he proved to be a very effective campaigner and fundraiser—both in 2008 and again in 2012—being president clearly required a range of leadership skills and tools that Obama had to learn on the job. With this background in mind, I've found some of President Obama's leadership traits especially interesting as they often cut both ways—meaning such characteristics can be seen as both positive and negative, depending on the situation. Consider the following cases.

Great Leaders "Need to Know"

The tendency to micromanage has been a major problem for other presidential leaders, including former president Jimmy Carter, who was such a notorious micromanager that he often had a hard time seeing the bigger picture. In fact, one often-told story about Carter as president was that he was so into the details of how the White House was being run that he personally assisted in approving the White House tennis court schedule. Apparently, he felt it was important that he knew such information and that he had the opportunity to veto certain people he felt shouldn't be on the court. The problem here seems pretty obvious: if a leader with such a huge portfolio of responsibility was engaged in an activity so small in scope as the White House tennis court schedule, what impact could this have on clouding his vision and his ability to keep the bigger picture of complex and difficult domestic and international affairs in mind?

President Obama has never been accused of such things. In fact, as a leader, Obama has developed the reputation as a "hands off" leader and a very strong delegator who trusts those around him to do what they are supposed to do. On the surface, this sounds benign. Yet, like any leadership trait or characteristic, when taken to an extreme it has the potential to cause problems. Take for example, the HealthCare.gov website, which was so critical to the implementation of the Affordable Care Act, or "Obamacare." This was the signature policy of the Obama administration, and the website was the key to the ultimate success of this healthcare reform effort, which Obama had worked on for years. It was supposed to be up and running on October 1, 2013. Yet, as discussed in detail in my chapter on leading change, there was every indication before the rollout that the website would not be ready on schedule and that those responsible, including Obama, were not on top of it. Ultimately, the website would go live with many glitches and limited functionality; the launch was a failure. In this case, President Obama needed to adapt his leadership style to become more engaged and involved and, frankly, more aggressive, with a real sense of urgency. The situation required a leader who would demand answers, have deadlines met, and who was willing to get involved in the details. That never happened—at least not until after it was already too late.

This hands-off leadership style is part of a larger pattern for President Obama, and it would also play a role in other significant shortcomings of the Obama administration, including the embarrassing scandal involving the National Security Administration and the surveillance of foreign leaders. When confronted, Obama acknowledged he was unaware of such an effort and was ultimately embarrassed on the world stage because of that lack of awareness. Yet, the question remains, why was he unaware? Should he have been aware? Would it have been micromanaging the NSA to have the people who were running the operation keep him abreast of their activities involving the surveillance of foreign leaders?

Another situation that once again caused significant embarrassment for the Obama White House occurred when the IRS targeted conservative groups by examining their tax returns for no apparent reason. The president's response? Once again, that he had no idea the activities were taking place, the same response he offered when the U.S. Embassy in Benghazi was attacked on September 11, 2012, and U.S. Ambassador J. Christopher Stephens and several other Americans were killed. Of course, terrible things can happen on a president's watch because the stakes are so high and the variables so great. However, as I think about the overall leadership approach and philosophy of President Obama, there seems to be a pattern in which the president simply says too often that he "didn't know" or seems not to have been as engaged as he should have been.

Mixed Signals

Further, there is the issue of perception of how engaged the president is. Part of a leader's job is to ensure those he or she is trying to lead know that he or she is "all in." Whether or not Barack Obama truly is all in, there have been times that the president seems to misunderstand the cues he is sending. One graphic and powerful example of this involved the tragic public execution and beheading of American journalist James Foley by ISIS. The president of course responded by condemning this terrible act in a press conference. Yet, while the president said all the right things, he sent another message entirely within minutes after this press conference when he was photographed smiling on the golf course. During an interview with Chuck Todd on NBC's *Meet the Press*, Obama explained, "It's always challenging when you're supposed to be on vacation. Because you're followed everywhere. And part of what I'd love is a vacation from the press."[1] While the country reeled from the graphic and horrifying images of an American being killed in such a fashion by terrorists who were clearly targeting U.S. citizens, it simply made no sense to play golf. The president had to know that as a leader, after such a horrible and tragic incident and so soon after his powerful words about the need to respond to ISIS, he simply couldn't go off and play eighteen holes of golf—and I'm an avid golfer myself.

Simply put, President Obama has many impressive leadership traits, including a calm demeanor, the ability to resist overreacting, and the ability to be composed and collected in difficult and intense situations. These are characteristics I particularly respect about President Obama as a leader. He doesn't take the bait when attacked. Consider how he handled the ridiculous and irresponsible charges Donald Trump made against him when Trump accused the president of not being a U.S. citizen. In response, Obama laughed, made fun of Trump, and ultimately, made Trump look foolish when documentation proving Obama's American citizenship was produced. Yet, my concern is that Obama can be so cool and hard to rattle that it often borders on being distant and causes him to seem disconnected from the things that matter most to the American people. It is just this kind of incident I described above, when President Obama was found on the golf course after holding a press conference about the beheading of an American journalist, that can cause many to conclude that he is in fact too detached. I'm not convinced that he is; rather, it's a matter of perception. What I mean by this is leaders need to have a clear sense of how their actions will be seen by those they are serving—those who need to be reassured and who need to know they are not just aware but engaged, involved, and committed to doing what needs to be done in the moment. It's not enough to hold a press conference and to say the right things about what needs to be done to ISIS. When he chose to go off and spend the day on a golf course, Obama's actions demonstrated a tone-deaf quality. The really great leaders understand these cues as well as the message being sent and shift their game plan.

The nation witnessed President Obama doing this in June 2015 after the horrific killings in a historic Black church in Charleston, South Carolina, which took the lives of nine people, including the church's pastor. President Obama delivered a powerful and emotional statement that offered his love and prayers for the community and for the families of the victims and shared his perspective on the all-too-prevalent issue of mass violence in America, stating that "It is in our power to do something about it." He demonstrated his caring and commitment further when he delivered a touching eulogy and speech at the funeral of the Reverend Clementa Pinckney, who had been gunned down during this horrific incident. In those critical moments, few leaders would have had the ability, empathy, and sensitivity not only to say the right thing but to do so in the right way, as President Obama had. Yet, again it is often confounding that the same person who can be so connected can also be so tone-deaf at other times as to the messages he's sending, which make him seem detached and emotionally disconnected.

This leadership lesson is less about politics or ideology and much more about what most people are looking for in the person leading them. Full disclosure: I voted for Barack Obama twice for president, but there have been many times that I have questioned how committed he really was to being the leader of our country in the second term. I don't know if the president was getting bored with the job after the 2012 election, but it sometimes seemed like he wasn't as engaged or as passionate as in the past. According to a *New York Post* analysis in July 2014, Obama played 81 rounds of golf in the first 628 days after he was reelected, a pace that would set him to double the 104 days he spent on the links during his first term.[2] Again, this isn't about politics but rather about the confidence those who are asked to follow Obama as the leader of the free world have in him when they are being sent such messages about how engaged or disengaged he is.

One of the most important lessons in leadership is that leaders can never lose the passion for the job they are doing. If that ever does happen, there is no doubt that it affects the leaders' ability to be effective in the leadership role. Either you're "all in" or you're not. It can happen to CEOs, football coaches, school principals, university presidents, and yes, presidents of the United States. Leaders can get tired, bored, or frankly sick of their job. There are the usual ups and downs, the peaks and valleys of being a leader. Perhaps Barack Obama has had enough of dealing with a Congress that he perceives to be blocking virtually every one of his initiatives—just because they are his initiatives and Congress doesn't want to see him succeed. I'm not saying that wouldn't be a normal or rational human reaction, but there is a huge lesson about leadership to be learned here. Obstacles and challenges are simply part of the job. They come with the leadership territory. Whether it is Congress blocking you or any other obstacle in your way, part of the job of being a leader is to confront these challenges head-on.

No one forced Obama to run the first time, and certainly no one forced him to run for reelection. As soon as he made that decision, he no longer had the option to become disengaged. The stakes are too high, the problems too great. There are too many people counting on him. Ultimately, being the president of the United States may often seem like a virtually impossible job. The same is true for the leader of any organization in difficult and challenging times. However, for those of us that choose this path, it is critical that the people we are asking to follow us believe we are 100 percent committed and nothing less. While President Obama has had many successes, and has been challenged as the first African American president in ways that no other president has, there have been too many times—from my perspective—that he simply hasn't been "all in," or as engaged or involved in the details of being president. Understandable, yes, but not acceptable—not for a truly great leader.

24

Great Leaders Deliver
Powerful Presentations

Is it an absolute must that a leader be a great charismatic speaker? Not necessarily. Clearly there are a lot of dynamic speakers who have little ability to lead an organization in any professional arena. Yet, after years of coaching in the very closely related fields of leadership and communication, I have concluded that in order to be a well-rounded, highly effective leader with the ability to motivate persuade and energize others, being able to present in a competent, cogent, and compelling fashion is critical. There are simply too many scenarios and too many situations where leaders have to present to a key audience or to important stakeholders. Leaders must be competent public speakers, particularly at annual shareholder meetings. Audiences at these meetings need to be convinced by a company's leader that things are moving in the right direction and, further, that they should keep their money invested, instead of abandoning ship because of negative press or rumors in the marketplace about problems at the company or an industry in trouble. What about the organizational leader who has to present to his or her board of trustees a sensitive or controversial decision that must be made and that needs the board's support in order to move forward?

Consider a CEO or COO who is holding a company-wide town hall meeting with employees to present a plan for a new policy or initiative that is likely to face opposition or resistance. These situations and so many others require that leaders be able to make a presentation that don't simply inform their audience but also motivates and inspires them convinces and engages them. You can inform people via e-mail, but as soon as you enter a public forum to discuss any important issue, any organizational or industry-related topic that is at stake, you are required to do so much more. I'm not saying you have to be another Martin Luther King Jr. or John F. Kennedy who speaks with soaring prose or makes a historic speech (the kind I discuss in chapter 25, about leaders who have made inspirational speeches). Yet, I have witnessed and worked with many leaders who have a massive gap in their professional tool kit when it comes to the ability to communicate with confidence, particularly in important public forums with a lot on the line. These leaders and their organizations have paid a hefty price.

Further, as chapter 15 discusses in detail, one of the most important roles of a leader is to advocate for change. The ability to do this is based in large part on your ability to present in a persuasive and engaging fashion. Think about it. A person in a leadership position can know all of the logical and strategic reasons for an organizational change but may lack the skills, tools, and insight to convince others as to why this change must take place. This critical leadership skill requires the desire not only to understand your audience but also to understand more about yourself. It also requires the desire to understand how you choose not just what you're saying but whom you're saying it to and what it all means. This demands a tremendous amount of emotional intelligence, which so many leaders lack, largely because they're unaware of the need to be competent in this area.

As I write this chapter, I am reminded of the time I sat in the audience at a recent corporate retreat while a highly paid leader in the healthcare field talked for hours about the strategic direction that a major healthcare organization needed to go in. This professional gave a presentation that completely reinforced for me just how critical it is for leaders to be effective presenters. Consider the following account of this retreat as an important lesson in leadership.

Data Dumpers Make Poor Leaders

A few months ago, I attended a corporate retreat of a large healthcare organization on the West Coast. My job at the retreat was to facilitate a conversation between the keynote speaker and an impressive audience of healthcare practitioners, including medical executives, physician leaders, nurse managers, and members of the board, as well as the senior leadership team.

Consider that the retreat—held over several days—was intended to discuss and make some tough decisions about the future of the host organization. The keynote speaker, considered a national leader in healthcare strategy, was asked to make a presentation at the retreat and provoke a vigorous discussion. Clearly, such a discussion and conversation about difficult challenges, issues, and questions was required in order to get closer to establishing the best strategic direction for this prominent healthcare organization. There was only one catch: the keynote speaker—a really pleasant guy—prepared and gave a PowerPoint presentation of 110 slides. *Yikes!* I'm not joking; he showed 110 detailed slides containing complicated and data-driven facts and figures. About one hour into this three-hours-plus presentation, it became obvious that the path the speaker took was all wrong. A leader must engage his or her audience. If your audience is not engaged, you can't inform them, much less motivate or lead them to move in a particular direction. They have stopped listening.

So, about one hour into this presentation, I looked closely at the audience of about 100 really impressive and important healthcare leaders, business executives, and trustees, who all had something meaningful to contribute to this strategic conversation. Yet, what I saw was a group of polite but clearly disengaged and very bored stakeholders. Many were on their smartphones, and some were nodding off. Others were working hard to pay attention to the key-noter but were turning the pages of his PowerPoint handout, trying to figure out when the heck the morning break would be coming. As for me—the facilitator of this healthcare retreat—I was pray-ing that this speaker would stop talking and pick up the obvious audience cues. I prayed that he saw he had lost them—big-time—with what he admitted was a highly didactic PowerPoint lecture. When it was all over, it would be my job to wake up the increas-ingly distracted audience and engage them in a Q&A session with the speaker about his ponderous presentation—which I could only hope some had paid partial attention to.

So what's the leadership lesson in all this? I call it the "but I have more slides!" phenomenon, which I wrote about in my book *Make the Connection*. This phenomenon plays out when a really smart professional in a leadership position misses the mark by a mile by thinking he needs to cram a massive amount of information into the heads of those in his audience. This is one way—a dictatorial leadership approach—to communicate information. What is so striking is that so many otherwise smart professionals in leader-ship positions do exactly the same thing. They are clueless about the need to create a more engaging two-way approach to sharing information—especially when attempting to move and motivate others. Can't they see that many of their audience members are falling asleep, walking out, playing with electronic devices—simply put, disengaged?

When we finally did get to the morning break, the entire discus-sion among the healthcare leaders at the retreat was about how bored they were. Some were angry, others were disillusioned, and I heard one head of a major surgical department say to a colleague, "That was a lot of information I never wanted or needed to know. What a waste of time." Being a great leader is not about being the person with the most information about a particular topic. Fur-ther, it is definitely not about being the "smartest person in the room," the one with the highest IQ. Rather, a great leader is the person who can engage, involve, and ultimately inspire his or her audience to participate in a difficult or challenging "conversation" while attempting to move them in a particular strategic direction. No person in a leadership position can do this while droning on, delivering a "data dump." Yet, leaders do just that every day while making presentations, running meetings, negotiating agreements, or simply talking one-on-one with important stakeholders.

A powerful lesson in leadership to remember: data dumpers ("but I have more slides!") make poor leaders. Conversely, people who engage their audience can create candid, strategic, and energizing conversations around pressing issues and questions and have the potential to lead the organization to greatness. With this in mind, consider the following case of the late governor of New York, Mario Cuomo, an extraordinary public orator who moved millions to tears with his words, passion, and iron-willed convictions.

Governor Mario Cuomo Moves Millions with His Words

In 2002, I was honored to have the opportunity to interview the late Mario Cuomo at the New Jersey Performing Arts Center in Newark. During this interview for public broadcasting, the fifty-second governor of New York, a giant in the world of American politics, discussed his career, his family, and the possibility of a presidential bid after his inspirational speech at the 1984 Democratic National Convention, which struck a chord with so many. These oratorical skills throughout his extraordinary public and political life are a large part of what made him a leader in the eyes of countless people. More than thirty years later, people still remember and talk about his speech and think about what could have been if Cuomo had chosen to run for the presidency. Although he didn't, his speech undoubtedly had a tremendous impact on America's political life.

I was especially excited to interview Mario Cuomo because, as a very young New Jersey state legislator, I was an elected delegate to the 1984 Democratic National Convention in San Francisco. On the night of his speech, I had left the New Jersey delegation to get closer to the podium and was in one of the first few rows in the convention hall for what has become known as the "Tale of Two Cities" speech.

I told him in our 2002 NJPAC interview how much his 1984 speech meant to me, and so many others, as if he hadn't heard that a million times already. I wanted to know how he prepared for the speech and if he knew he was making history as he was speaking. I must have sounded more like a starstruck fan than a professional PBS broadcaster. Yet, Cuomo was so forthcoming in our interview. He talked in detail about the Democratic National Convention speech, its aftermath, and why, despite so much support in the Democratic Party, he would twice reject a run for the presidency.

Cuomo talked about not really having the burning desire to do what was needed to run for president. Yet, he candidly explained that this "fire in the belly," as it was once described to him, was often more about ego and wanting something so badly for oneself. Instead, he was focused wholeheartedly on his commitment to New York and sticking with its citizens at a time they needed him the most (during a recession). Even without this "fire," Cuomo left so many following his speech in 1984 wishing he had in fact been the nominee. He also talked candidly about his battles with some leaders in the Catholic Church over his pro-choice stand, as well as his opposition to the death penalty and the price he paid for it in a heated, unsuccessful campaign for mayor of New York City in 1977 against Ed Koch.

The Cuomo interview was thirteen years ago, but it sticks in my mind like no other for me. He was candid, genuine, and articulate in a way that is hard to describe. (Ironic, I know.) I understood why he said he couldn't run for president, but I found myself then, and even more since his recent death, wishing he had come to a different conclusion. I'm not saying he was a perfect leader or governor, or that he would have been the perfect president. Too liberal for the country? Maybe. But there has always been a part of me, probably since I heard Mario Cuomo in San Francisco in 1984, that felt, given his extraordinary skills of persuasion, he would have been a special and unique president. He was the kind of leader that could inspire and challenge us to seek not just what was good for ourselves, but what was good for those around us who are struggling (a Pope Francis–like leadership quality). Also, maybe some of that was because he was a fellow Italian American—who really knows for sure?

But I believe it was more than that. Cuomo was more than that. He was a passionate and compassionate politician and leader. He was a once-in-a-lifetime public figure and a leader whose ability to connect with and make a lasting impact on his audience is something we can all learn from.

With this backdrop and context in mind concerning the importance of leaders delivering powerful presentations, consider the following six questions, which I use regularly when I coach and consult with leaders of all stripes as they prepare to make important presentations and game-changing speeches before audiences that really matter:

1 What is your main message to this audience?

If they forget everything else you say, what's the one thing you want to make sure they remember? You can't have three or four main messages. Most people can barely remember one. Edit yourself. Be disciplined in your communication. Everything you say in your presentation must support your main message. The key here is that you state the main message of a presentation in a clear, concise, and compelling sentence. This takes effort and focus as well as commitment to set the time aside—I suggest with key support staff—to discuss and debate this "message question." Get honest feedback. Consider possible messages and debate them back and forth. This investment in time and effort pays big dividends when you as a leader must stand and deliver in front of a challenging audience and present—with passion—a focused and compelling message. The biggest leadership lesson here is to never assume that your message will simply appear out of thin air—because it won't. And when it doesn't, while you're standing at that podium in front of an audience looking to you as their leader, you and your organization will pay a hefty price.

2 What will move, motivate, and inspire your audience? (It's about *them*!)

How will your message play with these people? Where is their passion? What does your audience feel passionately about? (You can't get people to care about what you are saying until they know you care about them.) What will get them to act? Once again, as a smart and aware leader, you understand that these critical questions need to be asked, not just by you but together with the best and brightest advisors. The leadership lesson here is to make these questions a part of your presentation preparation. Build the time to brainstorm and facilitate this important conversation that will help you as a leader to tap into your audience. Another important leadership lesson is to make sure that you talk to and engage several key people who will be in your audience before you actually present. Ask them these questions. It will help you as a leader see things from their point of view and will help you prepare and deliver a presentation that will have the maximum impact for your audience.

3 Where is your passion?

How do you really feel about the message you're delivering? Your audience needs to feel what you feel. I'm not talking about what you think, but what you *feel* on a deeper, more personal level. If an audience believes that you believe what you are saying, they are likely to be more receptive to your message, even if they don't agree with everything you say. Remember, it's not just having passion about your message, but being passionate about helping the audience you are attempting to connect with. Truly great leaders do not simply need to *know* what they are talking about when they are making a presentation— they need to *believe* it. They need to genuinely be passionate about what they are saying and *why* they are saying it. In many ways, this isn't really a leadership skill or tool. In fact, I've often thought that when it comes to passion, you either have it or you don't. Either you feel it or you don't feel it. Sometimes, in my career as an executive leadership coach, I've concluded that

I can't believe in someone's passion. In these instances, I'm not looking for leaders to feign passion that they don't feel; rather, I strive to pull out of them the passion that is lying dormant that they haven't tapped into yet. I often advocate that leaders must ask these challenging questions about what they really feel regarding what they are endorsing in a given presentation. So, if you're not feeling the passion, then ask yourself, "Why, exactly, should others be motivated to act or move in one direction or another just because I'm saying it?" A leader without passion who is making an important presentation about a challenging situation is like a soldier going into a critical battle totally unarmed. That soldier has very little chance of achieving his or her goal. So, once again, ask yourself, "If I don't truly believe in what I am presenting, why exactly should anyone else in my audience?" Not enough leaders ask this question of themselves before opening their mouths in very important venues when the stakes are very high.

4 Why not the status quo?

If you are proposing a new program or initiative, or anything that alters the status quo, what are the dangers of continuing the status quo (or put another way, why is there a sense of urgency to do anything different)? As a leader, you must understand that anything other than the status quo is often challenging for many people. It may even be unnatural. Therefore, a powerful leadership lesson is to consider why the status quo *won't* work. Make the case by using graphics and relevant examples of what is likely to happen if the present course of action is maintained. Further, make it clear that moving quickly with a genuine sense of urgency is vital. Again, paint a realistic picture of what the situation would be like if the team doesn't move in this direction. Great leaders paint powerful pictures to help their audiences understand and be moved to action.

5 What is the payoff?

Conversely, as a leader you must paint a positive picture of the good things that are likely to occur by investing the time and effort needed to accomplish what you are advocating in your presentation. It should come as no surprise that great leaders must present a positive uplifting message in order to get their team or organization to buy in. But this must be done by delivering specifics with concrete benefits. If you as a leader haven't figured out what these likely benefits and payoffs are, how can you expect others to buy into this decision? Therefore, an important leadership lesson is once again to invest the necessary time and effort to strategically identify the answers to these critical questions regarding the payoff for your people.

6 What's the call to action?

Tell your audience. Be specific. Once you've delivered your message in a passionate and personal way and you've tapped into the audience on a human level, it's time to close the deal. Don't leave people hanging. Give them direction and focus. Tell them exactly what you want them to do. Be specific in the action that you are proposing. If you aren't, you may create confusion and send mixed signals. That's right—the really great leaders close the deal. When it comes to presenting, a leader must cross the goal line—no field goals are acceptable, only touchdowns, which means a leader should assume nothing. Don't assume your people understand what they need to do to get the job done. Don't assume they are ready to execute the action that is needed. Tell them. Be directive. And don't feel that you are insulting their intelligence. Rather, you're helping them avoid any confusion. Never assume that the message sent is exactly the message that has been received. That's one of the most important leadership lessons to keep in mind when making a presentation. So be clear and be direct regarding exactly what the next steps are. The likelihood of successfully delivering an important message or implementing a policy change, new initiative, or whatever it is that has to be done will be much greater because of your efforts in this regard.

Finally, if you still find yourself asking, "How significant can a presentation really be?" I encourage you to read the case studies in the next chapter of three individuals who stepped up big on important stages and inspired millions in the process with their words, passion, and conviction. Great leaders do deliver powerful presentations.

25

Inspirational Speeches That Made a Difference

Consider the Gettysburg Address, Dr. Martin Luther King Jr.'s "I Have a Dream" speech, or President John F. Kennedy's inaugural address in which he said those memorable words, "Ask not what your country can do for you—ask what you can do for your country." There are many other memorable speeches made by well-known leaders, but every once in a while there is a speech made by someone in the most extraordinary of circumstances that stands the test of time—a speech that continues to be watched on You-Tube, moves people to tears, and motivates them in ways they had never imagined.

This chapter examines powerful and inspiring speeches by three special people in positions of leadership. All three speeches were given by leaders at the top of their profession who were also stricken with a terminal disease. All three leaders knew they were dying and chose to say and do something that would leave a mark—a legacy—when they were gone. One was a college basketball coach, another was a brilliant college professor, and the last was a baseball star known for his durability and strength; yet, all three leaders in very different venues gave speeches that would be talked about and referenced by leaders of all stripes to motivate others dealing with challenging situations and major obstacles for years to come.

Jimmy V's "Never Give Up" ESPY Speech

In March 1993, Jim Valvano, the former basketball coach of North Carolina State University, whose team had won the NCAA tournament a decade before, delivered one of the most powerful and memorable speeches while accepting the Arthur Ashe Courage and Humanitarian Award at the first televised ESPY Awards. Valvano was in the final stages of his battle with bone cancer—he died two months after his ESPY speech—and those in attendance knew that Jimmy V was likely making one of his last public appearances. He needed to be assisted to the podium by his two close friends and fellow coaches, Dick Vitale and Mike Krzyzewski.

In his speech, Valvano, who had lost a great deal of weight, came to life and was full of energy and passion, saying, "Time is very precious to me. I don't know how much I have left, and I have some things that I would like to say. . . . I'm fighting cancer, everybody knows that. People ask me all the time about how you go through your life and how's your day, and nothing is changed for me."

Valvano went on to say, "There are three things we all should do every day. Number one is laugh. You should laugh every day. Number two is think. You should spend some time in thought. Number three is, you should have your emotions moved to tears—could be happiness or joy. But think about it. If you laugh, you think, and you cry, that's a full day. That's a heck of a day. You do that seven days a week, you're going to have something special."

Valvano went on to talk about the Jimmy V Foundation for Cancer Research and the importance of raising money for cancer research. Said Valvano, "It may not save my life. It may save my children's lives. It may save someone you love. The Foundation's motto is 'Don't give up, don't ever give up.' That's what I'm going to try to do every minute that I have left. I will thank God for the day and the moment I have. I'm going to work as hard as I can for cancer research and hopefully, maybe, we'll have some cures and some breakthroughs."

Finally, with the crowd in tears and on the edge of their seats, Valvano concluded with this: "I gotta go, and I got one last thing and I said it before, and I want to say it again. Cancer can take away all my physical abilities. It cannot touch my mind, it cannot touch my heart, and it cannot touch my soul. And those three things are going to carry on forever."

Go on YouTube and check out Jim Valvano's ESPY speech. No PowerPoint slides. No charts. No graphs. Just an incredibly passionate, personal, and persuasive speech from the heart, from a leader who never gave up. Twenty-two years later, his words mean more than ever.

A Powerful "Last Lecture"

In the fall of 2008, a friend sent me a video that demonstrated in a powerful and dramatic fashion how one person can connect with millions in the way he communicates. The video was from an episode of *Oprah* featuring Randy Pausch, a professor at Carnegie Mellon University who had recently been diagnosed with incurable pancreatic cancer. Pausch, who was only forty-seven years old at the time, was told he had only a few months to live and decided that he would deliver what would come to be called "The Last Lecture." The father of three small children, ages five, two and one at the time, Pausch appeared to be the picture of good health, yet the multiple tumors in his pancreas made his prognosis painfully clear.

Professor Pausch delivered this memorable lecture in September 2007. Word had gotten to Oprah that his message was inspirational, and she decided to have him on her TV show. The presentation was titled "Really Achieving Your Childhood Dreams." Pausch decided that the topic of his "last lecture" would not be about dying, but rather about the "importance of overcoming obstacles" and "seizing every moment because time is all you have and you may find one day that you have less time than you think."

In short, Pausch's speech, which was being videotaped, was about celebrating life. Yet, while primarily intended for his students and colleagues at Carnegie Mellon, it was really so that his children would be left with powerful messages from their loving father.

What's fascinating from a leadership perspective is how Randy Pausch went about preparing this last lecture. He asked himself, "What do I, alone, truly have to offer?" and amassed hundreds of photos from his life as part of a PowerPoint presentation. He ultimately realized that only a few slides could be included, so he edited those photos and tied them to powerful messages.

He showed a giant slide of his CT scans, which had red arrows pointing to the many cancerous tumors that would ultimately take his life. Underneath this image was the caption "The Elephant in the Room." His presentation dealt with what he knew many in his audience were thinking about—his cancer and prognosis. But he quickly turned it around from a message about death to one about attitude and dealing with difficult circumstances. He said, "All right. That is what it is. We can't change it. We just have to decide how we'll respond." And then this PowerPoint slide: "We cannot change the cards we are dealt, just how we play the hand." What a powerful message about the nature of leadership as well as of life.

Pausch then put up a photo of his wife and his children in front of their Virginia home with the heading "I Am Not in Denial." His message to his riveted audience was that he clearly understood his dire circumstance and that it was impossible to be in denial with three small children who would soon be fatherless. He then put up a slide that read, "My Childhood Dreams," showing photos that matched some of those dreams, including "Playing in the NFL" or "Being Captain Kirk" or "Being a Disney Imagineer," all of which he succeeded in doing.

His presentation on Oprah lasted only ten minutes but had a lasting impact. Numerous audience members were moved to tears and clearly had experienced something they didn't anticipate. In Randy Pausch's "last lecture" he used extraordinary leadership skills to move, motivate, and inspire his audience. He also gave hope and a new meaning of life to those who have cancer, including terminal patients who may wonder what, if anything, they have to offer.

Pausch died in July 2008, but his "last lecture" lives on and demonstrates that one person in a position of leadership, through his words, passion, and message, can and sometimes does change the world, or at least how we look at life—and death.

"The Luckiest Man on the Face of the Earth"

Very few speeches stand the test of time, but July 4, 2014, marked the seventy-fifth anniversary of one such speech given by a dying Lou Gehrig at Yankee Stadium. Gehrig's "The Luckiest Man on the Face of the Earth" farewell address resonates as powerfully today as it did then for the tens of thousands who witnessed it in person, and the countless others who have heard and seen excerpts from it since.

After playing in 2,130 straight games over fifteen years, Gehrig, known as the "Iron Horse," was stricken with a debilitating disease that would end his playing days and, less than two years after this speech, his life. Gehrig knew he was dying. His teammates knew it, and the 60,000 fans in the stadium sensed it. Undaunted, Gehrig uttered these unforgettable words: "For the past two weeks you have been reading about the bad break I got. Yet today I consider myself the luckiest man on the face of this earth."

But it was the rest of what Gehrig said in less than two minutes that teaches us about what it takes to connect with so many under such difficult circumstances. Gehrig decided not to make the speech about himself. He talked about why he was so lucky "to have been in ball parks for seventeen years" and to have received so much "kindness and encouragement" from his fans. Then Gehrig turned to his teammates and said, "Look at these grand men. Which of you wouldn't consider it the highlight of his career just to associate with them for even one day? Sure, I'm lucky to have spent six years with that wonderful little fellow, Miller Huggins [his manager]. Then to have spent the next nine years with that outstanding leader, that smart student of psychology, the best manager in baseball today, Joe McCarthy. Sure, I'm lucky."

What touched so many about Gehrig's speech was his extraordinary humility. Clearly he was not "lucky." At thirty-seven, he was stricken with a fatal disease in the prime of his career. But he chose to focus on the positives. Instead of eliciting pity, he decided to say "thanks." He thanked the groundskeepers, and then turned to his family and thanked "a father and a mother who work all their lives so you can have an education and build your body." And finally, Gehrig thanked his wife, whom he called "a tower of strength—the finest I know."

Bringing tears to the eyes of thousands in the stadium, Gehrig concluded, "I may have had a tough break, but I have an awful lot to live for." Clearly, none of us would ever want to be in Gehrig's position facing a fatal illness, much less having to speak in front of a massive audience. But the lesson Gehrig taught us over seventy-five years ago is as powerful today as it was at the time. As a leader, regardless of the challenges you face, one of the keys to connecting with your audience is to make it about them. Gehrig talked about himself, but only in the context of how others treated him.

Lou Gehrig never called himself a leader—never sought the spotlight—but on this day he chose to deliver a positive, inspiring message that had nothing to do with baseball and everything to do with how one chooses to live one's life and face mortality. What we say in public—even in the most difficult and challenging circumstances—is a product of the choices we make. The great leaders know this instinctively. The choice that Gehrig made on July 4, 1939, was to leave others with a focus on the positive instead of pity for the victim. Easier said than done, I know. But that's what special leaders do under extraordinary circumstances, and that's how great speeches are made, and why sometimes they live on forever.

Notes

3. You Can't Lead Others Until You Learn to Lead Yourself

1. Albert Mehrabian, *Nonverbal Communication* (New Brunswick, NJ: Aldine Transaction, 1972).

2. Richard Carlson, *Don't Sweat the Small Stuff* (New York: Hyperion, 1997).

4. In Leadership (and in Life), Attitude Is Everything

1. Richard Carlson, *You Can Be Happy No Matter What* (Novato, CA: New World Library, 2006), 119.

2. Steve Politi, "Paralyzed Rutgers Football Player Eric LeGrand Still Has Something to Smile About," *NJ Advance Media for NJ.com*, April 26, 2011. http://www.nj.com/rutgersfootball/index.ssf/2011/04/politi_paralyzed_rutgers_footb .html.

3. Ibid.

4. Ibid.

5. Ibid.

6. Julia Spencer, *Looking through a Keyhole* (n.p.: Assistant Publishing, 2011).

7. Peter Gelzinis, "Dance Instructor Injured in Bombing Vows: 'I'll Dance Again' . . . and Run the Marathon," *Boston Herald*, April 22, 2013. http://www .bostonherald.com/news_opinion/columnists/peter_gelzinis/2013/04/dance _instructor_injured_in_bombing_vows_ill_dance.

5. It's About *Them*

1. Daniel Goleman, *Emotional Intelligence: Why It Can Matter More Than IQ* (New York: Bantam, 1995).

2. Barbara Kellerman, *Bad Leadership: What It Is, How It Happens, and Why It Matters* (Boston: Harvard Business School Press, 2004).

3. https://www.youtube.com/watch?v=cDDWvj_q-o8.

7. Listen, Really Listen!

1. Glenn Llopis, "6 Ways Effective Listening Can Make You a Better Leader," *Forbes*, May 20, 2013. http://www.forbes.com/sites/glennllopis/2013/05/20/6-effective-ways-listening-can-make-you-a-better-leader/2/.

2. Carol Kleiman, "Body Language Speaks the Loudest," *Chicago Tribune*, March 5, 2000. http://articles.chicagotribune.com/2000-03-05/news/0003050280_1_non-verbal-premier-auto-finance-interviewer.

8. Great Leaders Ask Great Questions

1. Marilee Adams, *Change Your Questions Change Your Life: 10 Powerful Tools for Life and Work* (San Francisco: Berrett-Koehler Publishers, 2009).

2. Ibid.

3. Ibid.

9. Great Leaders Build Future Leaders

1. Marty Brounstein, *Coaching and Mentoring for Dummies* (Foster City, CA: IDG Books Worldwide, 2000).

10. Receiving Feedback

1. "Silverman Leaves London Crowd Unamused," *NBC Today/Access Hollywood*, October 21, 2008. http://www.today.com/id/27298307/ns/today-today_entertainment/t/silverman-leaves-london-crowd-unamused/#.Vf71399Viko.

11. Leadership Is *Very* Personal

1. Jonathan Schuppe, "Cop Boss Takes on Blame for Turnout," *Star Ledger*, May 17, 2007. http://newarktalk.com/talk/viewtopic.php?t=8807&sid=e8a6c3d9364bb6cc0b41e05c2616bf68.

2. Ibid.

3. Rich Cimini, "Rex Ryan: No More Captains for Jets," ESPN, January, 3 2012. http://espn.go.com/nfl/story/_/id/7415765/new-york-jets-rex-ryan-says-think-had-pulse-team.

13. Pumping Up Your People

1. Jennifer Conlin, "At Zingerman's, Pastrami and Partnership," *New York Times*, July 5, 2014. http://www.nytimes.com/2014/07/06/business/at-zingermans-pastrami-and-partnership-to-go.html.

14. Getting the Wrong People Off the Bus

1. Jim Collins, *Good to Great: Why Some Companies Make the Leap . . . and Others Don't* (New York: HarperCollins Publishers, 2001).
2. Ibid.
3. Ibid.

15. Change Is the Only Constant

1. Spencer Johnson, *Who Moved My Cheese?* (New York: G. P. Putnam's Sons, 1998), jacket blurb.
2. Ibid.
3. Greg Botelho and Holly Yan, "Sebelius: Obamacare Website Problems Blindsided the President," CNN, October 23, 2013. http://www.cnn.com/2013/10/23/politics/obamacare-sebelius-interview/.
4. John Kotter, "Leading Change: Why Transformation Efforts Fail," *Harvard Business Review*, June 1995. https://hbr.org/1995/05/leading-change-why-transformation-efforts-fail-2.

16. Big Shoes to Fill

1. Michael Evans, "5 Steps to Create a Viable Succession Plan for Your Family Business," *Forbes*, August 28, 2013. http://www.forbes.com/sites/allbusiness/2013/08/28/5-steps-to-create-a-viable-succession-plan-for-your-family-business/.

18. Think You Know It All? Think Again

1. Michael Reuter, "Fill Your Life with Firsts," Three Minute Leadership, September 21, 2014. http://threeminuteleadership.com/2014/09/21/fill-your-life-with-firsts/.
2. Paul Vallely, "Where Pope Francis Learned Humility," *Atlantic*, August 23, 2015. http://www.theatlantic.com/international/archive/2015/08/pope-francis-cordoba-exile-humble/402032/.
3. Ibid.
4. Ibid.

19. Step Up and Take Responsibility, and Never Abandon the Ship

1. David Lipsky, *Absolutely American: Four Years at West Point* (New York: Houghton Mifflin, 2003).

2. Kevin Armstrong and Bill Hutchinson, "Tom Brady Finds Soft Landing Spot in First Appearance since Deflategate Report," *New York Daily News*, May 8, 2015. http://www.nydailynews.com/sports/football/brady-hears-cheers -appearance-wells-report-article-1.2214715.

3. Ben Jacobs, "Hillary Clinton Admits Private Email Server Was 'a Mistake,'" *Guardian*, September 8, 2015. http://www.theguardian.com/us-news/2015/sep/08 /hillary-clinton-apologizes-private-email-server.

4. Janet Hook and Reid J. Epstein, "Donald Trump's Insults Rattle Republican Rivals, Please Fans," *Wall Street Journal*, August 27, 2015. http://www.wsj .com/articles/donald-trumps-insults-rattle-republican-rivals-please-fans-1440632 659.

5. Michael Barbaro, "Buying a Trump Property, or So They Thought," *New York Times*, May 12, 2001. http://www.nytimes.com/2011/05/13/nyregion /feeling-deceived-over-homes-that-were-trump-in-name-only.html.

6. Janell Ross, "So Which Women Has Donald Trump Called 'Dogs' and 'Fat Pigs'?" *Washington Post*, August 8, 2015. http://www.washingtonpost.com/news /the-fix/wp/2015/08/08/so-which-women-has-donald-trump-called-dogs-and -fat-pigs/.

7. Elizabeth Chuck, "Baltimore Mayor Stephanie Rawlings-Blake under Fire for 'Space' to Destroy Comment," *NBC News*, April 28, 2015. http://www.nbc news.com/storyline/baltimore-unrest/mayor-stephanie-rawlings-blake-under-fire -giving-space-destroy-baltimore-n349656.

8. Randy DeSoto, "Baltimore Mayor Told Police to Stand Down, Leaving City Wide Open to Destruction," *Western Journalism*, April 30, 2015. http://www .westernjournalism.com/source-baltimore-mayor-told-police-to-stand-down -leaving-city-wide-open-to-destruction/.

9. Barbie Latza Nadeau, Holly Yan, and Greg Botelho, "Costa Concordia Captain Convicted in Deadly Shipwreck," CNN, February 11, 2015. http://www.cnn .com/2015/02/11/world/costa-concordia-trial/.

10. Elizabeth Flock, "Cruise Liner Captain Francesco Schettino Says He Abandoned Ship by Accident," *Washington Post*, January 18, 2012. http://www.wash ingtonpost.com/blogs/blogpost/post/cruise-liner-captain-francesco-schettino-says -he-abandoned-ship-by-accident/2012/01/18/gIQApK8x7P_blog.html.

11. Brian Ross and Megan Chuchmach, "Cruise Ship Disaster: Captain Released on House Arrest," ABC News, January 17, 2012. http://abcnews.go.com/Blotter /cruise-disaster-captain-claims-thrown-ship/story?id=15376275.

12. Flock, "Cruise Liner Captain Francesco Schettino Says He Abandoned Ship by Accident."

20. Leadership Lessons from JFK

1. Hugh Sidey, "The Lesson John Kennedy Learned from the Bay of Pigs," *Time*, April 16, 2001. http://content.time.com/time/nation/article/0,8599,106537,00 .html.

2. Ibid.

3. Ralph Martin, *A Hero for Our Time: An Intimate Story of the Kennedy Years* (Greenwich, CT: Fawcett Crest, 1984).

4. Gary Burnison, "JFK and the Absolutes of Leadership," LinkedIn, November 22, 2013. https://www.linkedin.com/pulse/20131122185352–281874400–12 -absolute-leadership-traits-of-john-f-kennedy.

5. Sidey, "The Lesson John Kennedy Learned from the Bay of Pigs."

22. Leadership Lessons from Lincoln

1. Doris K. Goodwin, *Team of Rivals: The Political Genius of Abraham Lincoln* (New York: Simon & Schuster, 2005), xvii.

2. Ibid., 723.

3. Steven Smith, "What Sort of Leader Was Lincoln?," *New York Times*, February 13, 2013. http://opinionator.blogs.nytimes.com/2013/02/13/what-sort-of-leader -was-lincoln/.

4. Ibid.

23. Obama as a Leader

1. Adam Edelman and Stephen Brown, "'I Should've Anticipated the Optics': Obama Admits Decision to Golf after James Foley Speech Was Mistake," *New York Daily News*, September 8, 2014. http://www.nydailynews.com/news /politics/anticipated-optics-obama-admits-decision-golf-james-foley-speech -mistake-article-1.1931030.

2. Ben Axelson, "Has Obama 'Checked Out' Early? Critics Point to 81 Rounds of Golf, Mansion Hunting in 2nd Term," *Syracuse Media*, July 28, 2014. http:// www.syracuse.com/news/index.ssf/2014/07/has_obama_checked_out_early_81 _rounds_of_golf_mansion_hunting_since_re-election.html.

About the Author

Steve Adubato, PhD, is a broadcaster, author, and motivational speaker. He has taught as a visiting university professor at New York University, Rutgers University, the New Jersey Institute of Technology, Seton Hall University, and Montclair State University. Steve is also an Emmy Award–winning anchor for Thirteen/WNET (PBS) as well as NJTV (PBS), and is a syndicated columnist focusing on leadership and communication. He regularly appears on NBC's *Today Show*, CNN, FOX, and NPR as a leadership expert and media and political analyst. Steve is the author of *Speak from the Heart, Make the Connection, What Were They Thinking?*, and *You Are the Brand*. He is married, the father of four children, and lives in New Jersey.